Love Transcended

Where Love Evolves into Consciousness

Vishwas Chavan

Vishwas

The characters and events portrayed in this book are fictitious. Any similarity to real persons, living or dead, is coincidental and not intended by the author.

ISBN-13: 978-93-341-8451-8 (ebook)
ISBN-13: 978-93-341-8195-1 (paperback)

Cover design by: Vishwas Chavan
Published by: Vishwas Chavan

Contents

Title Page	
Copyright	
Prologue	
The Tipping Point	1
The Road to Antara	6
What is Love?	12
Love vs. Lust	17
The Lotus of Love	22
Intimacy	28
Divine "Nope"	33
Vulnerability	39
Tantra	45
The Shiva and Shakti Within	50
The Mandala of Love	57
The Bridge of Words	63
Rituals of Love	69
Self-Love	75
The Healing Power of Love	81

Love and Creativity 87
Love Transcended 93
The Art of Living Love 99
Love as Liberation 105
From Retreat to Reality 110
Epilogue 117

Prologue

Why do seemingly unbreakable relationships eventually fall apart?

When did being intimate, which was once so natural, become such a battleground for expectations?

To what end are we so naive when it comes to love, given our level of education and experience?

For decades, these questions have been a quiet or loud voice in my head. Love is more than just a feeling, as I have learned the hard way along the winding road of my own life's adventure. This is the way. A practice it is. In the end, it's just a mental condition.

There is more to the ideas, theories, and techniques presented in "***Love Transcended: Where Love Evolves into Consciousness***" than meets the eye. I have devoted myself to the philosophy of love in all its holy forms, and it is a living, breathing reflection of my own experiences, my exploration of ancient wisdom, and my life. I have personally embarked on a path of discovery, learning, and, most importantly, unlearning, spanning the calm contemplation of Buddhist compassion to the passionate intensity of Tantric intimacy.

Without favoritism, fear, or the need for material possessions or external approval, I have learnt to love. Whether it's love for oneself, another, or the divine, I have fully embraced the sacredness of love. I have gained a deeper comprehension of the meaning of genuine love through my explorations of the tenets of OSHO, Tantra, Buddhism, and the ageless knowledge found in ancient writings. It was from this realization that this book was conceived.

However, this is not merely my story.

At a turning point in their lives, Advait, Ishaan, and Elina are all intertwined in a tale of love, loss, and awakening. True, their story is fictional, but only because the characters and settings are completely made up. Their problems, inquiries, and desires are genuine because they are reflective of the relationship problems, uncertainties, and desires that millions of people experience on a global scale.

Advait: The Master Who Knew Both Realms

For a long time, Advait was just like the rest of us: he wanted to prove himself in the scientific and academic communities. He became a renowned scientist, academic, and innovator despite coming from a modest middle-class background; he pursued education with unparalleled zeal. Knowledge, and the potential of science to bring about positive change, were his guiding principles.

However, disappointment followed each achievement. Moving up the ladder of scientific "innovation" and "education," he came to see that a large portion of it was a vicious circle perpetuated by a small group of intellectual gatekeepers, the so-called "heroes" of discovery. His eyes were opened to the fact that systems meant to encourage investigation were actually stifling it. He remained unfazed by this realization. It roused him.

Advait left the scientific elite and headed into the dense forests of the Western Ghats with an unwavering determination. There he established ***Antara***, a sanctuary for enlightenment, love, and personal development. Instead of being an ashram full of teachings and lectures, *Antara* is a place where people can meet their true selves and be led, not taught, by the peaceful knowledge of nature and Advaita's calming presence.

Science and spirituality are one in Advait. Instead of rejecting science, his teachings go beyond it, fusing rational thought with intuitive understanding. His mission in life is to remind people of something they may have forgotten: that true love comes from inside, not from outside sources.

Ishaan: A Goal-Seeker

In the busy Indian city of Pune, Ishaan's parents, Madhav and Mohini, raised him with a combination of kindness and discipline. His quiet ambition and intelligence were hallmarks of his time at Bishop's School. His goals were loftier than that of an Information Technology degree, which he pursued like many other young Indians with technological aptitude.

He traveled all the way to America, where he earned a Master's degree in computer science and landed a job at a famous Silicon Valley IT company. He met Elina, the woman who would alter the course of his life irrevocably, in the midst of the hectic world of deadlines and deliverables.

Elina: On the Search for a True Home

Elina spent her childhood in the peaceful countryside of Finland, where she encountered endless forests, perfect lakes, and the frigid, still nights of winter. Her childhood instilled in her the values of independence, perseverance, and inner fortitude. She is now the Human Resources manager at a tech company in the US, thanks to her academic journey that began with these qualities and ended with an MBA in Human Resources.

Ishaan was her soulmate, and they met across the globe from her family. The beginning of their love story was typical of contemporary love stories: full of the excitement of new experiences and the joy of being together. With the support of their families, they tied the knot, creating a union that others would be green with envy over. Their personalities were a perfect combination of cool Finland and warm India.

But love put them to the test, as it always does. With the arrival of their son, Ishlin, and the demands of their jobs and schedules, their once-easy love began to strain. They were led to London by their work transfers, who promised them a new beginning. In any case, the arrival of a new city did little to mend broken hearts. Months passed, weeks passed, and eventually, all they talked about was logistics: "Did you pick up Ishlin?" "Don't forget the client call at 9."Dreams were no longer discussed at midnight. Nothing left behind. No laughing together. Strangers they became.

Elina finally spoke out what they had been feeling but were too timid to express: "Ishaan, I can't do this anymore."

Inspiration for this Fictional Story

For some reason, I think a lot of people keep quiet about their relationship issues because they think they are "normal" or "inevitable." In the hopes that time would mend what love and action cannot, I have witnessed couples bury their animosity for years. For those individuals, this is the story. Dedicated to all couples out there, like Ishaan and Elina, who are in love but don't know how to express it.

Every reader can find a reflection of themselves in **Love Transcended**, which is more than just a story about Advait leading Ishaan and Elina back to themselves. You will face your own challenges, have your own questions, and maybe even find your own answers as you follow their journey.

Reading this story will make you reevaluate your views on love. *Love is more than just a feeling; it's a deep spiritual practice*, and this book will make you wonder. *Love is not something that can be "found" but rather lived out.* That is what this story will instill in you.

I have come to realize that *love is not something that can be owned.* An embodiment of this force is required. It is not a factor that exists independently of us. It is an innate quality that we discover.

Setting the Expectations

You will be exposed to enduring philosophies from Tantra, Vedanta, Buddhism, and Taoism through the conversations between Advait, Ishaan, and Elina. You will find both practical exercises and profound insights in each chapter, which draws upon ancient scriptures such as the *Metta Sutta*, and the *Vigyan Bhairav Tantra*, etc.

Nevertheless, it is not a "how-to" manual. This is not a talk. Imagine a conversation.

You will be led to: by following their narrative.

1. *Acquire knowledge of the distinction between attachment and love.*
2. *Love yourself again and learn to love as a way of life.*
3. *Strike a balance between being intimate and being lustful.*
4. *Harmonize the masculine and feminine aspects of one's relationship with another.*
5. *Reach a more transcendent and heavenly kind of love by letting go of your ego.*

In terms of relationships, this is more than that. The story explores the concept of love as a means of self-discovery.

Reading Ishaan and Elina's story will make you think about the relationships in your own life, both with people and with yourself. This story is for you if you are open to listening with all your heart, if you are ready to let go of old ideas about love, and if you are brave enough to look inside.

Love was always there, just like it was for Ishaan and Elina. Maybe you'll find it, too. It was ever-present, just waiting to be surpassed.

Love,

Vishwas

∞∞∞

The Tipping Point

A Call to Find Love Again

It was late October in London, and the air had the damp chill of all seasons. In their large, eerily quiet apartment, Ishaan sat across the dining table from his wife Elina, before untouched plates. Their three-year-old son, Ishlin, had already gone to sleep in his room, leaving the sound of a ticking clock to fill the emptiness. For months now, the tension between them had been bubbling to the surface, but tonight it would boil over.

"I can't keep doing this," Elina said softly, shattering the silence. Her voice sounded both tired and raw.

Ishaan looked up, startled. "Doing what?" he asked, even though he knew.

"This... this life that we're living," she said, gesturing vaguely. "It's as if we just...exist. You're so wrapped up in work, I'm drowning in mine, and we hardly even speak anymore unless it's about schedules or Ishlin."

Ishaan sighed and ran a hand through his hair. "This is very hard for you, I know, Elina. Only, this is simply — life, right?" We're both doing our best."

"Is it, though?" she retorted, her frustration rising to the top. "Ishaan, the strangers in our marriage have become each other. And it's not just a matter of time or labour — it's about us. Something is missing, something we've lost in the process... something important."

Her words crashed over Ishaan like a cold wave. He knew in his heart, she was right. The laughter, the intimacy, the dreams, and their happy relationship, had been so distant a memory. Between the demands of his tech entrepreneurship and her successful human resources career, they had become two ships passing in the night. Even the times they spent together were marred by unsaid grievances and unfulfilled desires.

"What do you want me to do, Elina?" he asked quietly, with a tone that is a mix of defensiveness and despair." "I do not know where to begin, and how to fix this?"

"I don't know, either," Elina said, breaking down. "But I know we can't continue like this."

Seeking Guidance

The following weekend, Ishaan and Elina decided to have an honest conversation about what to do next. They sat together in their living room, where Ishlin played with his toys nearby. They agreed not of blame, but talk of solutions.

"I don't want us to give up," Ishaan said. "But I also don't know how to fix what's broken."

"Maybe we need help," Elina said tentatively. "Someone who can show us the way, help us reconnect."

Ishaan nodded slowly. "Like counselling?"

"Maybe. Or something more..." Unearthly," she said, looking for the right words. "I feel like we need to know not only each other but ourselves. Why are we here, why have we lost our way."

As they put Ishlin to sleep that night, Ishaan felt a twist of hope and fear. Finally, for the first time in like a long time, they were on the same page that change was needed.

The next day, Ishaan rang his Baba (father), Madhav, back in Pune. Over a video call, Madhav sat on the other end as Ishaan vented — the fights, the silences, the sensation of growing apart. Never one to confide in anyone, Ishaan opened up completely.

"I don't know what to do, Baba," Ishaan said, his voice thick. "I think I'm losing her... losing us."

Madhav hesitated for a moment, then said. "Ishaan, you've made the first and most important move: noticing that there's a problem. Next is getting the right guidance. And I think I know someone who can help."

"Who?" Ishaan asked, leaning forward toward the screen.

"His name is Advait," Madhav said, a note of admiration in his voice. "He's an old friend, awesome man. He was a scientist, then an academician, and now he's devoted his life to helping people like you and Elina rediscover who they are and who they want to be together. He runs a retreat outside *Velhe* (in the midst of Western ghats, near *Pune*), in a village called *Sundervan*."

Ishaan frowned slightly. "A retreat? Is that what you think we need?"

"I realize it's not what you're expecting," Madhav said, "but Advait isn't your average counselor. He has a way about him that allows people to see things that they cannot see for themselves. He doesn't simply heal families; he changes lives. If you mean it, I will talk to him and see if he can take you."

A Leap Of Faith

Over the next few days, Madhav called Advait and explained to him about Ishaan and Elina. Advait, who was somewhat selective in whom he allowed into his abode, nevertheless agreed to meet with them, sensing the urgency and sincerity of their story. In early November, Advait confirmed their admission to the retreat, with the program scheduled to start in mid-December.

When Ishaan heard the news relayed by Madhav, he had a sense of relief tinged with apprehension. "Thank you, Baba. We'll make it work."

Elina was cautiously optimistic, too. "I guess this is it," she said one evening, sitting on their couch. "If this doesn't work..."

"It will," Ishaan cut in gently. "We have to believe it will."

The next few weeks were a whirlwind of preparation. Elina organized to delegate her work, and Ishaan created workflows to enable his team to function smoothly without him there. They made a reservation to fly from London Heathrow to Pune and worked with Madhav and Mohini (Ishaan's mother) to leave Ishlin in their care for the duration of the retreat.

As the time of their departure drew near, Ishaan and Elina were both feeling different emotions — hope, anxiety, and a distant tingling of a feeling they hadn't felt in a long time: possibility.

Departure From London

It was a cold morning in mid-December when Ishaan and Elina reached London Heathrow Airport together with

Ishlin. It was overcast, and a frigid wind blew through the terminal as they unloaded their bags from the cab. Ishaan settled the fare with the driver and Elina collected the tickets and passport.

The airport was filled with holiday travellers — families, couples and solo adventurers all on their way to destinations near and far. As they approached the check-in counter, Elina looked at Ishaan.

"Do you think we're doing the right thing?" she said, her voice gentle but laced with concern.

"I don't know," he admitted. "But I know we need to try. For us. For Ishlin."

Her expression softened, and she nodded. As they went through security and arrived at the gate, the enormity of what was to come started to dawn on them. This wasn't merely a trip; it was a turning point.

Sitting in the waiting area, Ishaan took Elina's hand. For the first time in months, she didn't withdraw. Their flight was called for boarding, and they shared a brief, hopeful smile. Whatever awaited them in India, they would face together.

∞∞∞

The Road to Antara

An Invitation to Begin

As Ishaan and Elina emerged from the arrival gate at Pune International Airport, each carrying a bag and their three-year-old son Ishlin safely tucked between them, the December air in Pune was shockingly frigid. The couple seemed quiet in spite of the festive mood; stillness that had become familiar over the past few years permeated their relationship.

"Over here!," a kind voice cried out. From across the throng, Ishaan's father, Madhav, gestured energetically. Beside him was Ishaan's mother, Mohini, whose grin was as brilliant as it always is. Ishlin started to laugh, wiggling out of Elina's hold to dash for his grandparents.

Madhav easily snatched the lad up. "There's my little champ!," he said, kissing the child's forehead. Turning his focus to Elina, he asked, "How was the flight?"

“Long but manageable”, Elina said, her Finnish accent softening her words. She quickly hugged Mohini, who stretched out to get her luggage.

Mohini remarked kindly, "It's so good to see you both," but her eyes stayed on her son, Ishaan. " Beta, you seem worn out."

Ishaan maintained a smile. "Just a small amount of jet lag, Ma. However, we are good."

"Well, let's get home," Madhav remarked, already headed for the car. "We have a delicious meal waiting; Ishlin could use some time to extend his legs."

The trip to Kalyani Nagar was short; the city hummed with energy. Their target was a two-story cottage constructed in the early 1990s, with softened whiteness walls from the vegetation of potted plants and creepers. The house was to Ishaan a storehouse of early memories. For Elina, it was a place of solace—a haven apart from their busy London existence.

Inside, the air smelled like freshly made cardamom flavoured tea. The family settled into the living room, a comfortable area with mismatched furniture and an antique wooden cabinet with family pictures from many years past.

Elina observed Mohini present a tray of appetisers before them. Elina replied, while having a fresh *Khari,* "this is exactly what we needed." "It's rather serene here."

"Enjoy it," Mohini remarked with a kind tone. "You two have been too busy. Your time is now to slow down."

Leaning back in his chair, Ishaan focussed his attention on his son, who was contentedly running a toy train on the floor. "We will be gone for a few days," he said, his voice hesitant. "Are you confident you will handle Ishlin?"

"Of course", Madhav said, stroking his son's shoulder. "We have raised you, haven't we?" He'll be fine."

Mohini spoke in response as well. "Besides, having some time alone will help two of you. Like a garden, relationships demand maintenance."

Elina nodded slightly in appreciation of the sentiment. "Thank you," she murmured quietly. "It means a lot."

An hour later, after ensuring Ishlin was settled with his grandparents, Ishaan stepped outside to the driveway where his father's brand new car gleamed under the afternoon sunlight.

"Drive carefully," Madhav said, handing him the keys. "The roads to Velhe can get tricky after dark."

"I will, Baba," Ishaan replied. "Thank you."

Elina followed Ishaan to the car. And, as she seated her fingers rested on the door handle. She turned back to the house where Mohini was standing at the driveway clutching Ishlin in her arms and Madhav at her side. "bye, Ma! bye, Baba!" Ishaan and Elina waived at all three of them - Madhav, Mohin and Ishlin.

The weight of the trip ahead sank between them as they pulled out of the driveway. Pune's recognizable skyline gave way to meandering lanes surrounded by verdant farmland and far-off hills.

The trip was generally silent, broken now by Elina pointing out the scenery. The Western Ghats loomed far-off, their tops covered in mist. Rolling down the window, Elina let the cold breeze over her face.

She broke the stillness, "Ishaan," and "Do you ever wonder about our path here?"

Glancing at her, he looked confused. "What do you mean?"

"I mean... us," she answered warily. "We used to have conversations about anything. We seem to be just managing each other right now."

Deeply inhaled, Ishaan tightened his grasp on the driving wheel. He said, "I know," "It's not like I'm not interested, Elina. Simply said, job, business, and even family all stack up. And I'm not sure how much more I should give than I presently do."

"It's not about giving more," Elina remarked gently. "It has to do with being here. With me. With us."

Ishaan ignored her words, and chose not to respond. Rather, he concentrated on the road as they neared Sundervan, a settlement tucked in thick vegetation.

Arrival At Antara

The sun was setting below the horizon by the time they arrived to *Antara*, the retreat venue, coloring the sky in orange and purple. Tucked up in a remote clearing surrounded by tall trees and the soft sound of a nearby stream, the refuge had a simple sign that read:

"Antara: A Space to Awaken."

Advait waited at the door with his saffron shawl elegantly wrapped across his shoulder. His calm demeanor and welcoming smile seemed to overcome the stress and tension in the air.

"Welcome," he said, his voice firm and low. "I presume, you are Ishaan and Elina?"

Elina stepped forward and answered, "Yes." "I appreciate you inviting us."

Advait motioned toward the retreat and added, "The journey here is just the beginning. Come let me help you to settle. There is enough of research to do."

An Invitation To Begin

Later that evening, they were seated in the courtyard of the retreat under a star-filled sky canvas. The air was chilly, the mood calm. Between them a little fire blazed, creating flickering shadows on their faces.

"What leads you here?" Advait asked, his eyes serene but sharp.

Elina hesitated then started to talk. "We are here because we have been struggling," she said. "Our relationship has lost something. It's hard to explain."

Ishaan then said, "Everything feels transactional." " Even love."

Avait nodded. “You have arrived at the right place. But tell me—what do you believe love is?”

Elina turned back to Advait after first looking at Ishaan. "I'm not sure anymore," she said. "I believe it relates to connection, but..."

“But connection is insufficient,” Advait said for her. "Love is not only a relationship. Wholeness is a condition of being that has nothing to do with what the other offers or absorbs.”

He hunched forward, his voice intensifying. "Love is not something to work at." You do not engage in it. *It is something you awaken within yourself*.”

Advait took up a little clay lamp off the table and turned on. "This flame," he declared, "represents love. Trying to hold it will burn you. Ignorance of it will extinguish it. *Love thrives in balance and harmony*.”

He said gently,

"यत्र नैव रागो न द्वेषो, तत्र तिष्ठति आत्मविदाग।"
Ytr naiv raagao n dveso, ttr tisthti aatmvidaaga.
(Where there is neither attachment nor
aversion, the soul resides in peace.)

"We will investigate this balance and harmony here, at *Antara,*" he stated. "Not to fix your relationship, but to awake yourselves."

The silence between Ishaan and Elina was not weighty with anxiety as they returned to their room. They experienced a fleeting hope for the first time in years.

∞∞∞

What is Love?

Beyond Desire and Attachment

As Elina and Ishaan entered *Antara*'s main courtyard, the morning mist still hung on the forested slopes. The calm sounds of a nearby stream produced a comforting tune while the air smelled of moist ground and flowering jasmine. Under a big banyan tree, Advait was seated cross-legged on a wooden platform. He appeared to be meditating, but his eyes opened, peaceful and inviting as they drew near.

"Good morning," Advait greeted the couple, his voice resonating with quiet strength. "I trust you rested well."

"We did," Ishaan replied, looking at Elina, who nodded. The discomfort of the previous day seemed to have softened, replaced by a wary curiosity.

Advait waved for them to settle on the cushions set out before him. "We start today. Allow me to probe you here. What, in your understanding, is love?"

Elina hesitated then reiterated the same that she opined last evening, "I believe it has to do with connection. About being present for someone."

Ishaan said, "And about commitment - effort. Love does not last without efforts."

Advait sighed softly. "Effort, connection, commitment—these are absolutely facets of love. Tell me, though, are they love itself or its derivatives?"

The couple cast perplexed looks at each other. "What do you imply?" Elina questioned.

The Lamp And The Flame

Advait reached out on the platform next to him for a little bronze lantern. Lighting it, he sandwiched it between them. "This lamp marks love," he stated. "The flame gives warmth and light; it is consistent. But picture if I could grab it firmly with my hands." He stopped, staring straight back at both Elina and Ishaan. "What might happen?" he questioned.

Elina replied quietly, "It would burn you."

"Exactly," Advait replied. "That is what attachment does. It kills the very thing it is trying to hold by mistaking the flame for something to own or something to possess."

He leaned forward. "And what if I were to place this lamp in a storm?"

Ishaan responded, "It would extinguish."

"Desire is that storm," Advait stated. "It is endless, insatiable, always demanding more, limitless and hungry. It makes love flicker and falter. *Attachment grasps - desire consumes.* Neither lets the flame of love burn continuously and steadily."

A Sage's Journey

"Let me share something from my own life," Advait began in a contemplative tone. "Once like you, Ishaan—driven, aspirational, and captivated by the idea that love was something to reach, like a goal. I had a partner, a wonderful woman who matched my quest for greatness and intellectual curiosity. Though we created a life together, something was always lacking. We mistakenly confused attachment with love and desire for connection."

He stopped the far-off gaze in his eyes flickering with anguish. "I was hurt when she went. Not because I loved her selflessly but rather because her absence distorted my view of myself. It was at that point I started to doubt and question everything. What kind of "love" did I believe I had mastered? Why had it failed?"

Elina and Ishaan listened intently; the vulnerability in Advait's voice drew them in.

"I turned to the knowledge of old books," Advait said. "One verse from the *Bhagavad Gita* transformed everything for me:

'काम्येषु न रमते यः, स ब्रह्मनिष्ठः।'
(**Kāmyeṣu Na Ramate Yaḥ, sa brahmaniṣṭhaḥ**.)
("***The one who is unattached to desires finds peace in the eternal.***")

He paused, allowing the words to sink in. "It was not love that had failed me, but my understanding of it. *Love is not something to grasp or demand - it is a state of being. It is not found in another; it is awakened within.*"

The Tale Of The Lotus

Advait smiled, and with a softening tone said, "Let me tell you a story. In a far-flung kingdom, a young prince was mesmerised by the beauty of a lotus blooming in a pond. Driven to possess it, he waded into the water and plucked it, only to discover its petals were withering in his hands.

Disappointed and heartbroken, he sought the advice from an elderly monk."

"The lotus blooms not for you but because it is rooted in the mud and fed by the water," the monk told him. "Never pluck it if you want to enjoy its beauty. Instead tend to the pond."

Elina tilted her head thoughtfully. "So the pond is our inner world?"

Advait remarked precisely. "*Love is the lotus, and it blooms only when the pond—your inner self—is clear and nourished.* When your heart is burdened by attachment or clouded by desire, the lotus withers."

Wisdom From The Metta Sutta

Advait turned to look at the horizon and continued in an even softer voice. "The Buddha spoke of loving-kindness in his *Metta Sutta,* and I quote."

"As a mother protects her only child, so should one cultivate boundless love toward all beings."

Advait continued further. "This love is not possessive. Such a love asks for nothing in return. It flows freely, touching, healing, and inspiring everyone it encounters."

"But how can we cultivate that kind of love?" Ishaan asked intending to overcome his skepticism.

"By beginning with yourself," Advait added. "The first step is *self-love*—not the luxurious type, but the acceptance of who you are, flaws and all. You release others from the burden of completing you when you stop seeking validation from others."

Practicing Awareness

Advait closed his eyes for a moment, then opened them calmly. "Let us try something basic," he said. You close your eyes. Get deep in your breathing. Feel the love within you widening with every inhale. With every exhale, release the craving for control or possession.

Elina and Ishaan did as instructed. The experience seemed to hold profound wisdom, despite its silence.

"Love begins here," Advait whispered gently, shattering quiet. "Not in what you give to another but in what you awaken inside yourself."

As the session came to an end, Advait looked at both of them with gentle encouragement and a smile. “Think about this.” Advaid continued. “Are you picking the lotus or tending to the pond? Are you caressing the flame or are you holding it too tightly?”

Elina and Ishaan looked at each other, their regular tension replaced by something unspoken—a shared sense of possibilities.

Rising elegantly, Advait continued, "Next, we will explore the obstacles preventing us from truly experiencing love. Let these questions help you till then.”

As she strolled back to the room, the words of *Metta Sutta*'s echoed Elina's mind *"May all beings be happy. May every beings be free from suffering.”*

She thought, for the first time in years, that freedom and happiness were seeds just waiting to blossom rather than far-off fantasies.

∞∞∞

Love vs. Lust

The Thin Line

The sun was rising higher in the sky as Elina and Ishaan approached the shaded pavilion where Advait waited for them. Wildflowers, followed by the crisp smell of bees and burnt over-head. Even among the tranquility of *Antara*, though, there was a tightness in Ishaan's posture, an undercurrent of tension in his body language that was almost the opposite of Elina's peaceful surroundings.

Advait met them with his trademark calm smile. "Good morning," he said, waving for them to sit. They met today instead of the courtyard but under a wooden gazebo by a small lotus pond. The flowers floated peacefully on the surface of the water, their beauty magnified in stillness.

After a moment's silence, Advait asked, "What do you know about the word 'lust'?"

Ishaan arched his brow, taken aback by the question being so direct. I guess it's... physical attraction," he said after a pause. "Desire for someone."

"And love?" Advait prompted.

"What?" Ishaan faltered, glancing at Elina for strength.

Instead it was her answering, her voice soft. "Love feels...

deeper. It's about connection, not simply desire."

Advait nodded. "Love and lust are both natural experiences. However, the difficulty is in the understanding of what they are and how to differentiate one from the other. Let me tell you a story that might help."

The Butterfly And The Flame

Advait readjusted the shawl draped around his long shoulder and, in a voice with a cadence that may have been a metaphor for the pond he held, continued.

"There was a butterfly who lived, long ago, in a forest like this one. Its wings were a glimmering tapestry of colors under the sunlight that captivated all eyes that fell upon it. One evening, while the butterfly flew near a village, it saw a flickering flame in the window of a hut. Fire's flicker was hypnotic, its glow seductive.

'This is a wonderful strange thing that glows so beautifully.' the butterfly wondered. It flitted near, orbiting the flame. The warmth was reassuring, the light heady.

But as the butterfly approached, its wings began to singe. It was pained but called it passion. 'Must be the love I have waited for,' thought the butterfly. It soared even nearer, lost in its longing. In a moment of amorous blindness, it dove into the flame and never emerged.

A monk standing nearby, watching the whole thing, whispered to himself, 'How often do we, like the butterfly, confuse the lure of the flame for the light of love?' "

Ishaan and Elina were on a high level of feel, so Advait paused and drove that story deep into their throat. "The flame my friends, is lust — burning, consuming, ephemeral. The blind desires of the butterfly turned pain into pleasure. And so, it perished."

The Nature Of Lust

"Lust is like the flame," Advait went on. "It's a volatile force. It's a force that, if you're not aware of it, will charge forward in a strong way, be driven with intensity, urgency, and with a desire to devour without looking back. It centers on the seize-able, the ownershipable. But *love is the sun: steady, nurturing and infinite. Its goal is no longer to devour but to enlighten.*"

"But aren't you physically attracted to someone you love?" What do you mean?" Elina asked, her brow furrowed. "It's how a lot of relationships start."

"Indeed," Advait replied. "Nothing inherently wrong with attraction. It is a portal, but not the goal. The trouble is, we confuse the door for the house."

He looked at Ishaan. "Tell me, Ishaan, when you feel attracted to somebody, what happens in your mind?"

Ishaan shifted uncomfortably. "It's... hard to explain. It's as if my thoughts are stuck on them. "It's like I want to feel them close, to reach out to them."

"Precisely," Advait said. "Lust narrows the mind. It takes on a singular importance and can blind us to the person's essence. Love, on the other hand, stretches your mind. It allows us to see the other as they are, without the urge to own or dominate."

The Vedic Perspective

Advait nodded to the lotus pond. "According to the

Vedic tradition, the *Purusharthas*, or four aims of life, provide guidance. These are *Dharma* (righteousness), *Artha* (material pursuits), *Kama* (desire), and *Moksha* (liberation). *Kama*, or Desire, is not denounced; it is a part of life. The next path of life must be in and follow the progressive pattern of *Dharma* and free the *Moksha*."

He quoted a verse from the *Bhagavad Gita*:

'ध्यायतो विषयान्पुंसः, सङ्गस्तेषूपजायते।
(Dhyāyato viṣayānpuṁsaḥ, saṅgasteṣūpajāyate.)
('When a person dwells on objects of desire, attachment to them arises.')

"It is this attachment," he said, "that converts desire into bondage. We forget the spiritual when we chase only the physical."

Love As Connection

Elina spoke again, hesitantly. "So how do we develop beyond lust? How do we allow love to take its rightful place?"

Advait smiled. "By cultivating awareness. Lust is reactive — it pushes you outward. Love, by contrast, is inward-facing — it pulls you in. When you stop, breathe and recognize your intentions, you start to notice the difference."

"It's not the love that you consume." said Advait. "It honors the other as they are, not as you want them to be. Lust usually says, 'What can I take? Love asks, 'What can I give?' "

A Practice For Awareness

"Let's try a simple practice," Advait said, changing

his posture. "Shut your eyes and concentrate on your breathing. Take a deep breath, picturing a light filling your chest. As you breathe out, let go of any sense of needing or wanting. Take slow breaths and let your mind quiet."

Elina and Ishaan obeyed his command, their breaths syncing deeper. And for the first time, they were caught in the stillness of the moment, and instead of becoming quiet, the outside veils, the outside fog, became clear.

It was a few minutes later that Advait piped up again. "Every time you are overcome with desire or distracted by physical attraction, come back to your breath. It is your anchoring, your path back to awareness."

At the end of the session, the kind eyes looked back at Advaita. "When lust and love are enemies, they are teachers. *Lust reveals what we want; love reveals what we need. When you align the two with awareness, they are not in conflict — they harmonize.*"

Elina and Ishaan sat for a while in silence, the ripples on the pond a reflection of what they were feeling. Walking back to their room, Ishaan turned to Elina. "It's strange," he said. "I've always viewed love and lust as opposites. But maybe they're just different legs of the same journey."

Elina nodded, brushing her hand with his. "Maybe this is our beginning. Not to divide the two, but to make sense of them."

The lily pads on the pond dipped in the wind, their roots entangled among the muck while their flowers sought the sun.

∞∞∞

The Lotus of Love

Discovering the many facets of Love

The next morning, golden light streamed through the dense canopies of *Sundervan*, dappling sunlight on the retreat's stone walkways. Elina and Ishaan quietly walked towards the central hall, their steps slower than the previous days. Somehow, the air at *Antara* called for stillness, a kind of pause starting to untie the knots of tension they brought.

Advait welcomed them at the entrance, his face calm. But today, rather than take them to the large courtyard that was open to anyone who would stop by the House, he directed them towards a small circular chamber with wide windows overlooking the tree line. Cushions were placed in a half-circle around a low wooden table on which sat a single flower — a lotus.

"Today's session," Advait started, sitting cross-legged, "is on comprehending the multiple facets of love."

Ishaan raised an eyebrow. "Dimensions?"

"Yes," Advait said. "*Love is not singular. It is wide, a river with many tributaries.* "Romantic love, platonic love, the love of a parent for his or her child, the love for the divine — they each flow in different directions, but they all trace back to the same source."

Elina frowned and tilted her head to the side. "So, are they all... the same?"

Advait smiled. "They are various expressions of the same essence. Let me show you with the stories of three people — a mother, a lover, a friend."

The Love Of A Mother: A Tale Of Selflessness

He gazed at the floor, and began, his voice unwavering and metered, as though plucking it from the estuaries of reminiscence.

"There once lived a woman named Kaveri who was from a small village at the foot of a mountain. She was a widow, raising her young son on her own. They were living a simple yet happy life. Kaveri would wake up every morning before dawn to work in the fields so that her son could be fed and go to school.

"One year, there were no monsoons, and the crops dried up. Kaveri faced a choice: sell the last piece of jewelry she had — her wedding necklace — or pull her son out of school to save money. She sold the necklace, without a second guess.

"When her son grew older and able to comprehend the sacrifice that she had made, he asked her, 'Why did you give up something so precious?'

"Because *love is not about what we hold on to — it is about what we are willing to let go of,*" Kaveri replied. "

Advait hesitated, looking from Elina to Ishaan, then from Ishaan to Elina. "This is what a mother's love is all about. It is not transactional. "It asks for nothing in return, yet it gives it's all."

Elina's eyes welled up when she remembered their son, Ishlin, back in Pune with his grandparents. "I think I see that sort of love in Ishaan's parents," she said gently. "All to support Ishlin, and us."

"Indeed," Advait said. "*Parental love is a love that tells us to sacrifice. It is a reflection of the divine — a love that protects without condition.*"

The Lover's Love: A Dance Of Passion And Vulnerability

Advait straightened up and started another story.

Once there was a poet called Arman. And he fell in love with a dancer called Amira. It was hot and passionate and all-consuming. Arman penned verses about Amira's gentleness, likening her to moonlight reflecting on a placid lake. Amira, in turn, was inspired by his words, her dance infused with a beauty she didn't know she had.

"But one day, Amira confided to Arman, 'I worry that you do not see me. You are so much like me; you only see your own desires reflected in me.'

"Arman was deeply moved by her words. He understood that his love had been more about the concept of her than her actual self. That day, he traded in his pen for an ear. He listened to her stories, to her fears, to her dreams. "A fire doesn't consume, it lights over time — their love evolved.

Advait looked at Ishaan. "Romantic love is a game of passion and vulnerability — between what you reveal, and what you withhold. At its outset desire drives it — but in order for love to endure, it must be transmuted into understanding."

Ishaan shifted uncomfortably. "But isn't wanting someone

part of love?"

"It is," Advait said. "But that is just the start. Desire is the spark; vulnerability is the fuel. *True love starts when we no longer see the other one as an object of our desire but as our own humanity.* "

Friend's Love: A Bond Without Demands

As he entered the third story, Advait's tone softened.

"In a faraway land, there were two friends, Maya and Veda, who grew up together. They were symbiotic and shared every joy and sorrow. Maya then one day had decided to leave their village and go to the work to unlock her fortune in a distant city. So Veda stayed on, caring for her family's farm.

"They hadn't seen each other for years, but they were writing back and forth constantly. Then one year, no letters came anymore. Maya, who had gotten very busy with her new life, forgot to write. Then one day, completely unexpectedly, she got a package. In it was a plain scarf and a note that said: 'I still think of you every time the wind brings the scent of jasmine.'

Maya cried as she understood that true friendship doesn't require attention or closeness. It just is — like the sky, which is there even when the clouds hide it.'

Advait leaned forward. "I think friendship teaches *love doesn't always need to be reciprocated. It lives in the silences of expectation.*"

The Universal Nature Of Love

Advait pointed to the lotus pond just outside the window.

"Do you see how the water nourishes the lotus? The lotus does not bloom for the water. It simply flows, giving life. Such is the nature of love, in whatever incarnation — parental, romantic, platonic and even spiritual. When not burdened by demands, it flows freely."

He went on, "In the *Tao Te Ching*, it says:

'The sage does not cling to love; thus love clings to him.'

"This means that love is a lot like water — it cannot be contained, it cannot be controlled." "When you let it flow naturally, it nourishes everything it touches."

A Practice: Opening The Heart

"Now, Advait said, "let us do something simple. Close your eyes."

Elina and Ishaan complied, their breathing gradually reducing with each of Advait's instructions. "Visualize a small stream running from your heart. As you inhale and exhale, let it grow. Imagine it getting to someone you love. Now let it spill out to one who is hard to love. Finally, let it come down to you."

For a moment, the only sound was leaves rustling in the wind outside. When their eyes opened, both Elina and Ishaan seemed to feel lighter, as if some invisible burden had been lifted.

"Love is not a single thing," Advait said as he stood smoothly. "It has many faces, but its spirit is the same. It is the thread that links us to ourselves, to each other and the divine."

While walking back to their room, Ishaan grasped Elina's hand. "Perhaps we've tried to make love one thing," he said.

"But it's more than that. It's everything."

Elina smiled. "Perhaps it's time we let it flow."

The lotus flowers floated on the pond within a sway of the breeze, their petals glistening in the morning sun, an unassuming reminder of the universal and infinite nature of love.

∞∞∞

Intimacy

A Journey to the Soul

As they stepped into a quiet pavilion at the fringes of the retreat, the afternoon sun poured a sheet of gold over *Antara*. It was warm; but the air smelt of sandalwood, and the soft rustle of leaves was a soothing background. Advait was waiting for them, perched on a low cushion with a brass bowl full of rose petals in front of him. It was the same penetrating gaze but a lighter mood today.

"Welcome," he said, motioning for them to take a seat. "Today we dive into intimacy — not in the world's view, but as a divine expedition to the soul."

Elina looked at Ishaan, intrigued. "Intimacy is... closeness, isn't it?" she asked.

"All that, yes," Advait said. "But it's much more than proximity of bodies. *True intimacy is the joining of two souls—unfiltered, vulnerable and maskless.* It takes courage, because it requires vulnerability."

Ishaan raised an eyebrow. "Vulnerability? That sounds like a weakness."

Advait smiled faintly. "It's often mistaken as such. But let me tell you a story that may help you see differently."

The Potter And The Vessel

"There was a potter who was known in his village as the maker of the prettiest clay pots and pans. One day, an apprentice said to him, 'How do you make these pots so perfect? The potter gives to the apprentice some clay and tells him, 'First make it soft.'

"The apprentice labored hard, beating and kneading the unyielding clay, but to no avail. Lastly, the potter picked up the clay and poured water into it before he started to knead it with gentle and rhythmic strokes. In a while, the clay has given way, pliably.

"'Softness is not weakness,' the potter said. 'It's the first step to becoming something beautiful. If not, the vessel will crack long before it is ever fired.' "

Advait looked at Ishaan. "*Vulnerability is, like, softening the clay. Without it, intimacy is shallow—delicate and easily shattered.* But when we have the courage to be vulnerable, we become able to create something lasting."

The Essence Of Intimacy

Elina leaned in, a pensive look on her face. "But how can we open up like that? How do we break down the walls we've built over the years?"

"So she is…" Advait nodded to confirm her query. "Intimacy starts with presence. Being with another without judgment or agenda opens a space: a sacred space where both of you can be as you are, without pretense."

He pointed to the bowl of rose petal in front of him. "In the *Kamasutra*, intimacy is a form of art — something you do for devotion, not just for sex. Every petal a layer of ourselves — some beautiful and fragrant, others bruised and tucked away. To be intimate, he explained, is to invite another to witness all your layers and to witness theirs in response."

The Role Of Tantric Practices

Advait became more reflective in his tone. "In *Tantra,* intimacy is far more than just the body. It is about merging energies. "With true intimacy between two people, there's a sacred union there, where 'I' and 'you' is no more."

He cited the *Vigyan Bhairav Tantra*:

"सर्वं देहगतं द्रव्यं, चित्तगं तन्मयो भवेत्।"
(Sarvam dehagatam dravyam, chittagam tanmayo bhavet.)
('All that is within the body, and all that is within the mind, becomes one in the act of conscious union.')

"This union," Advait said, "is physical but it's also emotional, spiritual, energetic. This means that when you are fully present with another, when you're not just two people but mirrors for each other's souls."

Proven Tactics For Connection

Advait adopted a more matter-of-fact tone. "Let us practice something," he said. "This is an ancient practice from the world of both *Tantra* and modern mindfulness traditions. It is simple but profound."

1. The Eye-Gazing Exercise:

"Sit opposite each other," Advait said. "Close enough that your knees are nearly touching. Now gaze into one another's eyes — not to analyze or judge, but merely to bear witness. "See the person in front of you as they truly are, not as you want them to be. Maintain this gaze for at least five minutes."

Elina and Ishaan hesitated but complied with his command. It was awkward at first, their eyes darting with unease during the silence. But then something changed as seconds became minutes. Elina looked past Ishaan's furrowed brow and tired eyes; she saw the vulnerability that he kept hidden. Even Ishaan began to recognize the magnitude of Elina's love, masked by her frustration and despair.

When the exercise was over, Elina dried a tear. "I saw ... you," she said quietly. "Not the busy man only, the provider. I saw you."

Ishaan nodded, his voice heavy. "And I saw you — not the complaints or the hurt, but the woman who believed in us enough to bring us here."

2. Heart-to-Heart Breathing:

"Now place your right hand on one another's heart," Advait said. "Close eyes, synchronize breath. With every inhale, feel you're breathing in each other's energy. As you exhale, release fear and judgment."

As their breaths fell into sync together, the room seemed to melt away. No past, no future — only the present moment, sacred and shared.

The Courage Of Intimacy

Once the exercises concluded, Advait spoke up. "Intimacy is not for the faint of heart. It takes the bravery to be fully witnessed — and to fully witness in kind. It's not about perfection; it's about acceptance."

He recited softly,

"यत्र यत्र चक्षु दृष्टि, तत्र तत्र आत्मा स्थितः।"
(Yatra yatra chakshu drishti, tatra tatra atma sthitah.)
('Wherever your gaze rests, there your soul is present.')

"Bring this presence with you when you interact," he said. "May intimacy be a space for your souls to meet and not just your bodies or your words."

An Invitation To Deepen

Walking back to their room that night, Elina had asked Ishaan. "I've never been that close to you before. It wasn't easy, but... sky was real."

Ishaan nodded, his fingers grazing hers. "Maybe we should have been too busy to fix things not to notice each other."

"Maybe intimacy isn't about fixing," Elina said, thoughtfully. "Maybe it's about moving on."

The stars above *Antara* twinkled fiercely, as if the first step towards a deeper connection between the couple were being witnessed.

∞∞∞

Divine "Nope"

The Power of Boundaries

The mid-morning sunlight poured into *Antara*'s library through latticed windows, its rays casting intricate patterns on a polished wooden floor. Philosophy, mindfulness and spirituality books lined shelves around the room, and a brass pot of fresh tulsi leaves sat on a small table in the center. Advait planted himself at the head of the table, hands loosely folded, and Ishaan and Elina settled down across from him.

"Today," Advait started, "we're talking about something that I think gets glossed over but that is critical to love and intimacy: boundaries. Tell me, what does the word mean to you?"

Ishaan thought for a moment. "Boundaries ... I suppose they're about keeping things in check. Protecting yourself."

Elina nodded. "And protecting others, too. But sometimes it feels difficult, like saying no can hurt someone."

Advait smiled gently. "It is hard, of course, but *without limits love becomes vague. It loses its power, its clarity earthiness*. Let me share a fable from ancient Buddhist lore that serves to shine a little light on this."

The Prince & A Hermit

"There was a young prince whose kindness was legendary. He bestowed freely on all who came to him, gold, land, food. His people loved him, but his ministers became worried. "If you give without limits," they warned, "the kingdom itself will run dry."

"The prince, however, brushed off their fears. 'How could I deny anyone who needed it?' he replied.

"One day the hermit came to the palace. He went to the prince and said, 'Your Highness, I need your support. Would you come with me to the woods and be my attendant for a year?"

"The prince agreed without a moment's hesitation, to the horror of his ministers. The prince worked for a year in the forest carrying water, chopping wood and serving the hermit. At year-end, the hermit said, 'I have taught you the greatest lesson of all: the importance of boundaries.'

"Perplexed, the prince said, 'But I served you loudly complaining. 'How is this a boundary lesson?'

"The hermit smiled. "By agreeing to help me, you neglected the kingdom. Unlimited philanthropy is just as dangerous as unlimited capitalism. Just as the river can only flow between two banks, *love and kindness can only flourish when there are healthy boundaries*." "

Advait paused and allowed the story to settle in their minds. "The prince learned that a *NO is not a rejection of love — it is an affirmation of balance*."

The Wisdom Of *Sila*: Ethics — The Making Of A Civil Society

"Boundaries are part of *Sila*, or ethical discipline, according to Buddhist teachings," Advait explained. "The *Pali* texts tell us that discipline is not about making ourselves miserable, but about freedom — freedom from harm and guilt and ever-present overload."

He quoted a line from the *Dhammapada*:

"सच्चं न परिहानन्ति, धर्मं पुञ्ञं च साधुते।"
(Saccaṁ na parihānanti, dhammaṁ puññaṁ ca sādhute.)
('Truth and discipline protect those who honor them.')

Advait went on, "Boundaries are an act of truth — to self and to others. Is when we say no that we honor our capacity and allow love to grow where it can."

But many don't recognize why they're not enough in so-called modern relationships.

Elina leaned forward. "But how do we set boundaries without being... selfish? It's easier, sometimes, to just say yes, even when it hurts.'"

"That's the paradox," Advait said. "Agreeing when you don't want to do something might seem nice in the moment, but it breeds resentment in the long run. Boundaries are not walls you build to keep others out; *boundaries are bridges you build to guarantee mutual respect.*"

He turned to Ishaan. "Usually in your work, you have deadlines and objectives. Could you allow every client to set your schedule?"

"Do I? No," Ishaan answered. "There has to be structure."

"Precisely," Advait said. "And so it is about relationships. "*Without structure, without boundaries, love is chaos.*"

Boundary Setting: Practical Tips

Advait grinned to himself, heading into practical advisement. “Let’s learn how to set boundaries in a way that nourishes and does not harm.”

1. Identify Your Limits

"Take a few minutes to think," Advait said. What are the things you need - physically, emotionally, spiritually - to feel balanced?"

"Setting boundaries begins with knowing your limits." he continued, offering an exercise. (a) List 3 things that are most important to you in a relationship, (b) Write 3 things that exhaust you, and (c) refer these lists when thinking about where to enforce or draw the boundaries.

2. Communicate with Compassion

"Boundaries are not about rejection," explained Advait. "They are about clarity. While communicating your boundary, focus on conveying your feeling, and not attempting to accuse the partner.".

Exercise: Instead of saying, "You're always late and disrespectful", try to say, "I feel disrespected when schedule is not maintained. Can we work on being punctual together?".

3. Learn to Say NO

"Saying NO is not easy, but it is necessary at times" said Advait. "The key is to say it with love and compassion, and not hostility."

Practice saying NO: for instance,

"I'd really like to help, but I am not available right now.",

"I have to spend sometime with myself today, can we reschedule?"

"These responses," Advait explained, "validate your boundaries, without hearting or isolating the other person."

4. Ritual to Affirm Your Boundaries

"In Tantra," Advait said, "tools are applied to open sacred spaces. Rituals can be used to create boundaries in your relationships."

Example Ritual: Allocate 10 minutes each day to self-reflection without any distractions. During that time, do breathing exercises or journal your thoughts. Perform this ritual with your partner, inviting them to respect this sacred space as well.

The Courage To Honor Yourself

Advait got up and pointed to the forest beyond the retreat. "Do you see those trees? Alone they are tall and separate but together they make a forest. Their roots do not intertwine; they are respectful of one another's space. This is what boundaries accomplish — they enable us to grow apart and yet be connected.'"

He recited softly:

"यत्र धर्मं प्रतिष्ठितं, तत्र प्रेमं प्रवर्तते।"
(Yatra dharmaṁ pratiṣṭhitaṁ, tatra premaṁ pravartate.)
('Where discipline resides, love flows.')

An Invitation To Practice

At the end of the session, Advait smiled at both of them.

"Tonight, practice saying no — not to one another, but to something you feel takes energy from you. Notice how it feels. Consider how the gesture made you feel, did it bring you peace or discomfort? This is the first step in creating sacred boundaries."

When they turned to walk back, Elina replied, "To be honest I've always thought saying no is a rejection. But perhaps it's a way to preserve what matters."

Ishaan nodded thoughtfully. *"Boundaries aren't just for keeping others out, they are for keeping ourselves intact."*

The sun went down, and Antara was cloaked in shadows. The couple's conversation, while quiet, had a newfound clarity — an understanding that saying no might, at times, be the most loving thing of all.

∞∞∞

Vulnerability

The Key to Authentic Love

It was a still night at *Antara,* the usual rustles of crickets and leaves hushed by the cold still of the December air. Elina sat upon the bed's edge in their room, simple yet comfortable, idly tracing the embroidery of the cushion on the side. Ishaan was sitting at the window, staring at the star-clad forest. In a place so calm, there seemed a heaviness in the room — muted expectation of the day's session with Advait.

"This ... is a lot," Ishaan finally said, facing Elina. "All these stories, these practices — it's like they're asking us to peel back layers I never even knew I had."

Elina nodded. "Maybe that's what it's about," she said quietly. "Maybe we've been protected by those layers for too long. And the walls we create ... "

The Morning Session

The following morning, Advait received them once more in an open pavilion, where a breeze wafted the smell of marigolds. And today, in between them, sat a clay pot, its surface embellished with intricate designs. There was a single crack running down one side, faint but visible.

“Tell me,” Advait said, his tone steady, “what do you think of when you think of vulnerability?”

“It’s... exposing yourself,” Ishaan added after a pause. “Revealing parts of you that you’d like to keep hidden.”

“And why are we hiding those parts?” Advait asked.

“To protect us,” Elina cut in. “Of being judged, hurt, or rejected.”

Advait nodded. “Indeed. Vulnerability feels like weakness because we have a fear of what might happen if we are fully seen. But let me tell you a story that might change how you view that.”

The Story Of The Healer

“Once, there was a healer, Priya,” Advait began, his voice constructing a story as vivid as the light of the morning. "Her skill in healing people's ailments—from broken bones to fevers—was well-known in her village. However, Priya kept a secret—a childhood scar that extended down her back, concealed under layers of clothing and silence—despite her achievements.

"Even those who wanted to love Priya kept their distance because she was so embarrassed by her scar. The village boy broke his leg one day, and Priya's remedies weren't sufficient. She sought out the assistance of a different healer, a wise old lady from a nearby town.

“The old healer lady saw Priya's guarded expression as she arrived. The wise old woman then turned to Priya and asked, "Why are you bearing this burden?" after attending to the boy.

"Priya paused, then gingerly lifted her shirt to expose the scar. 'This scar is not your shame; it is your story,' the wise old lady healer said with a smile. "It reveals not where you were broken, but where and how you survived."

"When Priya finally spoke up, she felt the burden of her silence ease. She came to understand that being vulnerable actually strengthened her by bringing her closer to others."

Advait held his breath, allowing the tale to linger. "Having a scar, like Priya does, does not make her weak. True love, the kind that doesn't shrink from flaws, is woven from this thread."

The Courage To Be Seen

“But isn’t vulnerability risky?” Ishaan asked, sounding skeptical. “What if someone uses that to their advantage?”

“True vulnerability isn’t about letting it all hang out,” Advait answered. “It really is about who you choose to be seen by. It is a gift, not a gamble.”

He went on, “According to the teachings of OSHO, vulnerability is the courage to lower your guards and allow love to flow without a leash. When we hide behind walls, we keep others out, but we also imprison ourselves inside.”

He quoted softly,

"जहाँ भय समाप्त होता है, वहीं प्रेम का जन्म होता है।"
(Jahaan bhay samapt hota hai, wahin prem ka janm hota hai.)
(‘Where fear ends, love begins.’)

The Mirror Of Vulnerability (Private Ritual)

That night, Advait asked Elina and Ishaan to do a private exercise in their room. "This is a ritual of self-acceptance," he said. "It's going to feel like a lot, but that's where growth starts — at discomfort."

The Exercise: The Vulnerability Mirror

***Step 1**: Preparation:* Find a large mirror in the room — a place that's secluded and away from distractions. Light a candle for a soft, sacred atmosphere.

***Step 2**: Self-Reflection:* (a) Stand in front of the mirror and study yourself — your face, your body, your posture. Do not judge; simply observe., (b) Say out loud one truth about yourself that you've been afraid to face. It might be a fear, a regret or a secret dream.

***Step 3**: Partner Reflection:* (a) Sit facing each other. One person starts and speaks about something that makes them feel vulnerable, and the other listens without interrupting or responding., (b) When one of them ends, the other replies, "Thank you for sharing. I see you."

***Step 4**: Affirmation: The ritual ends with you standing in front of the mirror with your partner, holding each other's hands. Say the affirmation: "We are whole, even in our imperfections."*

The Practice In Action

That night, Elina managed to light a candle in their room, her hands quaking slightly. "Are you ready for this?" she asked Ishaan, who nodded, but looked just as uncertain.

She spoke first as they faced the mirror. "I... I'm afraid of not being good enough," she confessed, her voice little more than a whisper. "Not good enough as a wife, as a mother, not even as me."

Ishaan reached for her hand. "I have always felt you were more than enough," he said. "But I suppose I've never told you that."

It was Ishaan's turn, and he paused. "I'm scared of failure," he said at last. "Of not being the man you or Ishlin need me to be. I hide behind work, because ... it's easier than saying out loud that I don't always have the answers."

Elina squeezed his hand. "You don't need to have all the answers," she said. "You just have to show up."

And as they looked at each other in the mirror, the fear of the unspoken pains that use to hang vaporous in the air between them, did vanish. They had looked at each other for the first time in years — not as roles to play, but as two flawed, reflective people choosing to love one another in all their imperfection.

The Freedom Of Vulnerability

The following morning, Advait heard their story with a smile. "Vulnerability is not about fixing what's broken," he said. "It is about accepting what is. If you accept your errors, you allow others to accept theirs, 'When you are okay with your imperfections, you allow others to do the same."

He quoted a verse from the *Vigyan Bhairav Tantra*:

"अपि दोषाः विभात्यन्ते, प्रेम्ना भवति निर्वृतिः।"
(Api doṣāḥ vibhātyante, premnā bhavati nirvṛtiḥ.)
('Even flaws become radiant in love, for love transforms all into peace.')

Continued Advait: "When you allow yourself to be seen,

you create a space for authentic love to flourish—a love that is not based on fear, but on freedom."

Later that evening, as they strolled through the gardens, Ishaan said to Elina. “It was weird, standing there and saying those words out loud.” But it also felt… freeing.”

Elina smiled. *“Mabe vulnerability isn’t a sign of weakness. Maybe it’s about being real.”*

Ishaan nodded. “And maybe that’s what we’ve been missing — seeing each other for our true selves, and not who we think we ought to be.”

Above them, the banyan trees swayed gently in the breeze, their roots entwined with the earth—a quiet reminder of the strength that comes from grounding oneself in truth.

∞∞∞

Tantra

Transforming Love Into Liberation

The noon sunlight basked *Antara* in warm golden glow; Ishaan and Elina stood beside Advait at the venerable banyan tree. Today's session had a different feel to it — Advait's eyes held a quiet intensity, as if something deep was about to go down.

"Today," Advait began, "we enter a domain in which love moves beyond the personal to be a path to liberation. The Essence of *Tantra*."

Ishaan frowned slightly. "Isn't Tantra mainly about ... you know, intimacy and rituals?"

Advait chuckled softly. "That is the common misconception. *Tantra* is not for people who want to indulge; it is for those who want to transcend. It weaves the material with the etherical into one harmonic flow. Welcome to its roots through the story of *Shiva* and *Shakti*."

The Story Of Shiva And Shakti

"In the old Himalayan valleys," Advait started, "the sages would often share the story of *Shiva* and *Shakti*, the universal lovers. *Shiva is pure consciousness, the impassive, changeless reality. Shakti, energy, the active principle of*

Creation. Shiva, without Shakti, is passive, and Shakti without Shiva is disorganized. But together they make the dance of existence."

He stopped, and pointed to the far hills. "One day, *Shakti* went to *Shiva* and said, 'You sit there quietly while I am creating endlessly. Without you, I am restless. Without me, you're not even alive.'

"Only as an observer I am nothing without you,' *Shiva* said. Your energy is aimless without me. We are the universe itself, together.'

"And thus, *Shakti* danced for *Shiva,* her dance vibrant and graceful, and *Shiva* meditated, anchoring her energy. Their union was more than physical — it was the joining of opposites, the balancing of stillness and motion, of the masculine and the feminine, of the finite and the infinite."

Elina and Ishaan looked at Advait. Tangentially, "This is *Tantra: the alchemy of opposites coming together, where love is our path to freedom — not by avoiding the body but by going deeper into it."*

The Misunderstanding Of Tantra

Advait leaned forward. "The world has misunderstood the essence of *Tantra* as just physical practices. But *Tantra* is so much deeper. It doesn't despise the body; it reveres it as a temple." It doesn't turn away from desire; it uses desire as a doorway into the divine."

He softly quoted part of the *Vigyan Bhairav Tantra*:

"सर्वं देहं चित्तं च, शिवं च शक्तिसंयुतम्।"
(Sarvam dehaṁ cittaṁ ca, śivaṁ ca śaktisaṁyutam.)
('The body, the mind, Shiva, and Shakti—when

united, they become the sacred whole.')

"*Tantra* teaches us that *love is not something to flee but something to deepen. The soul is reached through the body. We only transcend it through desire.*"

Breathing To Balance, A Practical Exploration

Advait helped them get seated comfortably. "We will do *Pranayama* — breathing techniques which balance the masculine and feminine energies — in order to know the union of *Shiva* and *Shakti* in you."

The Breathing Practice

Preparation: *Nadi Shodhana* (Alternate Nostril Breathing): (a) Find a comfortable seated position, with a straight spine., (b) Close your right nostril with your thumb, then inhale long and slow through your left nostril., (c) Using your ring finger, close off your left nostril, release your thumb, and exhale through your right nostril.

Repeat for 10 cycles, alternating nostrils with each breath.

Purpose: Balances the energies of *Shiva* (masculine, logical) and *Shakti* (feminine, intuitive).

Visualization: The Heating Power

(a) Now close your eyes and put your hands on your lower abdomen.,

(b) Take a deep inhale visualizing warm, golden light emanating from the base of your spine (*Shakti*).

(c) Visualize the light flowing into your heart center

(*Shiva*) as you release it with your exhale.

Repeat for five minutes.

Purpose: Opens energy channels and connects physical and spiritual.

The Sacred Union (Private Ritual)

Advait asked Elina and Ishaan to do a ritual that night in their room to deepen their bonding and embody the teachings of Tantra.

Set the Space: (a) Burn candles or incense to set a calm mood, and (b) Face each other and touch knees, and put a single flower between you.

Breath Synchronization: (a) Start by gazing into one another's eyes, keeping the gaze uninterrupted by words, and (b) Begin to breathe together in unison, matching the rhythm of your inhales and exhales.

Heart Connection: (a) Put your right hand on each other's heart, and (b) See as your breath comes into their chest and connects there like two rivers.

Affirmation: (a) Take turns staring into each other's faces and saying, "I see you. I honor you. I love you as you are.", and (b) Let the words flow naturally, without expectation.

Close the Ritual: Sit in silence, hands clasped, sensitive to the shared energy.

The Dance Of Shiva And Shakti

The following day, Advait learned from Elina and Ishaan of their experience of last night's ritual. "It was...

intense," Elina said. "It was awkward at first, but then it transformed. It was as if we weren't just two people — we were... connected."

Ishaan nodded. "I felt that too. It wasn't just about us. It felt... bigger."

Advait smiled. *"That is the dance of Shiva and Shakti. When you connect deeply, you cease to be "you" and "I." You are a reflection of the cosmic union, where love moves beyond the personal and into the divine."*

He gave a verse from the *Kama Sutra*:

"योगिनः कर्मसंधाने, स्नेहं शिवं च तन्मयम्।"
(Yoginaḥ karmasaṁdhāne, snehaṁ śivaṁ ca tanmayam.)
('When actions align with love, the union of Shiva and Shakti is realized.')

Advait ended the session with this thought. "*Tantra* encourages you to perceive love not as a passing emotion, but as a transformative force. It neither dismisses the body nor confines itself to it. Instead it leads you to the beyond where love is liberation."

So, as Ishaan and Elina ambled back through the gardens, the words ran around in their head. They felt lighter, as if a veil had been lifted — not only between themselves, but inside themselves.

Above them, the boughs of the banyan tree reached up some height, a living embodiment of the marriage between earth and sky, *Shiva* and *Shakti* — a gentle reminder that love is not just a path, but a destination.

∞∞∞

The Shiva and Shakti Within

Balancing Masculine and Feminine Energies for Inner Harmony

The afternoon sun hung low in the sky, casting long, dappled shadows across the banyan tree's dense canopy at *Antara*. Ishaan and Elina reached the small circular pavilion, curiosity brimming in them — Advait's cryptic words from early that morning ringing in their ears: "Today, we go out to explore the sun and the moon you carry within you."

As they eased themselves down on to the cushions, they saw two symbols drawn with chalk on a slate board, in front of Advait. One was a shiny sun, bright and brazen. The other was a crescent moon, calm and gentle. A flowing line connected them, joining the two in harmony.

Advait started to speak, his tone even but firm, "*The masculine and feminine are not about gender. They are energies, polarities that we all carry within. The sun and the moon. Shiva and Shakti. Yang and Yin. When balanced, they create harmony. In their unbalanced form, they cause conflict.*"

The Sun And The Moon

"There is an old tribal tale," Advait said, his voice weaving the story into the stillness of the afternoon. "In a realm long before the universe we know, the Sun and the Moon were siblings, born of the same cosmic mother. It was a bright and deep Sun. The Moon was mellow and curative, walking coolly through the night.

"One day, the Sun bragged, 'I am the giver of life. 'Without my heat and light, nothing would live.'

"The Moon said, 'Your fire may create life, but my stillness allows life to slumber.' There can be no balance without me."

"Their argument heated up to the point where their mother had to intervene. "You're both right," she said. 'And both wrong. The Sun's energetic force must be moderated by the Moon's calmness, and the Moon's coolness must be vivified by the Sun's heat. You make the rhythm of life together. Alone, you are incomplete.'

"And thus the Sun and the Moon learned to live together, their tugging and pulling creating the tides, the seasons and the dance of life itself."

The Masculine And Feminine Within Us

Advait waited, staring between Ishaan and Elina. "This is not just a story about the cosmos — it is a story about you. The Sun embodies masculine energy: doing, logic, structure. The Moon represents the feminine energy: our intuition, emotions and flow. Masculine and Feminine are both needed; most of us live in imbalance."

Ishaan frowned slightly. "Imbalance? How do you mean?"

"In today's society," Advait said, "the Sun generally eclipses the Moon. We are trained to prioritize doing over being, thinking over feeling, structure over fluidity. But whenever one energy dominates, we lose our center."

He gestured toward Elina. "For instance, you might stretch yourself too thin to nurture others while denying yourself boundaries — an excess of the feminine resulting in the imbalance of the feminine. And you, Ishaan, may become consumed by work and logic, so that you lose touch with your emotional core — an imbalance of the masculine."

Elina nodded slowly. "I've felt that imbalance. As if I'm overextending and losing myself in the meantime."

Ishaan sighed. "And I've felt... detached. You know, as I always do but never really feel it."

Advait smiled gently. "Awareness is the first step. "Now, let us see what we can do to balance these energies."

The Taoist Concept Of Yin And Yang

"In *Taoist* philosophy," Advait went on, "the masculine and feminine are known as *Yang* and *Yin*. *Yang* is the Sun—active, assertive and expansive. *Yin* is the Moon—receptive, reflective, nurturing. *Tai Chi,* the eternal dance of opposites creating harmony."

He traced the classic Yin-Yang symbol in the sand, a circle divided by a flowing line, each half containing a dot of the other. "Notice the dots," he said. "They help us remember that in any masculine energy, there's a seed of the feminine, and the other way around. *"A balance is not equality—it is harmony."*

Advait quoted softly,

"तत्र शान्तिः यत्र संतुलनं।"

(Tatra shāntiḥ yatra santulanam.)
('Peace resides where balance exists.')

Balancing Energies: A Practical Exploration

1. Morning Sun Salutation (Awaken the Masculine)

"Let us start with a practice to activate your masculine energy," Advait said.

The Practice: 10 rounds of *Surya Namaskar* (Sun Salutations), strong, deep movements. Inhale the energy of the Sun with every breath. On each exhale release tension and ground yourself.
Purpose: Brings on the active, configured energy of masculine.

2. Evening Moon Meditation (Embrace the Feminine)

"Now, we will celebrate the feminine with a soothing meditation," Advait said.

The Practice: Find a space that is quiet and dimly lit. If you want, close your eyes and imagine a silver moon over your head, its light soaking through to your body. Inhale slowly, feeling its cool, healing energy.
Purpose: Accesses intuition, emotional discharge, invitation to be open.

3. The Circle of Balance (Shared Practice)

"This is something you can do together," Advait told Elina and Ishaan.

Step 1: Sit in front of each other and hold hands.

Step 2: First, the masculine energy (Ishaan) speaks and sets an intention: “I offer my strength and presence.”

Step 3: The more feminine energy in the group, Elina, replies: “I bring my intuition and compassion.”

Step 4: One person repeats these affirmations, hearing the words; the other person feels the words.

Purpose: syncing partners energy to w respect and connection but not dependence.

Advait's Story: Life Out Of Balance

Advait leaned back, his expression thoughtful. “I was once like the Sun—constantly striving, achieving, burning bright but exhausting myself. My days as a scientist were filled with logic and action, but I ignored the Moon within me. It wasn’t until I began studying *Taoist* and *Tantric* practices that I understood the need for balance.”

He paused, his gaze softening. “One night, while meditating under a full moon, I felt something shift. I realized that strength without softness is brittle, and intuition without direction is aimless. That was when I began to heal—not by rejecting one energy, but by integrating both.”

As the session ended, Advait recited a verse from the *Tao Te Ching*:

"The masculine protects; the feminine nurtures. Together,

they create life. Separate, they wither."

He added, "Tonight, reflect on where your energies are imbalanced. Where are you overextending? Where are you holding back? Awareness is the key to harmony."

The Dance Of The Sun And Moon (Private Ritual)

That evening, in the privacy of their room, Elina and Ishaan performed a ritual Advait had suggested.

> **Step 1**: Light two candles—one gold (representing the Sun) and one silver (representing the Moon).
>
> **Step 2**: Stand facing each other. Ishaan began by circling Elina, moving with strong, deliberate steps, embodying the Sun's energy. Elina then mirrored his movements with soft, flowing gestures, embodying the Moon.
>
> **Step 3**: Gradually, they synchronized their movements, creating a fluid dance that felt both structured and free.
>
> **Step 4**: They ended the ritual by sitting together, their hands intertwined, breathing deeply in unison.

When the ritual was complete, they felt a profound sense of balance—not just within themselves, but between each other.

The Path To Harmony

The next morning, as they shared their experience with Advait, Ishaan said, "I felt... centered. Like I wasn't just the one driving everything. There was a flow."

Elina added, "And I felt like I could be soft without losing myself. It was freeing."

Advait nodded. "That is the essence of balancing the masculine and feminine. When these energies are in harmony, you stop struggling against yourself. You move with the rhythm of life."

The sun and moon, though far apart, shared the same sky above *Antara*—a quiet reminder that balance is not about separation, but integration.

∞∞∞

The Mandala of Love

Awakening the Chakras to Cultivate Love

As they walked into *Antara*'s meditation hall, the crisp morning air perfumed by blooming jasmine. Today's session was different from the rest; you could feel an unspoken energy in the space. The center of the room was occupied by colourful mandalas depicting the seven chakras, each signifying a specific persona.

Advait acknowledged them with that serene smile of his. "Welcome. Today, we are taking you on a journey of love — not just as an emotion, but as an energy that travels within you, shaping your mind, body, and spirit."

The Tale Of The Villager's Healing

Advait sat cross-legged and started telling the story.

"There lived a man called Suryan in a small village by the banks of the river Godavari. He was a farmer, strong of body but broken of spirit. Years of struggle had made him callous, and he became estranged from his family and friends.

"One day, an old sage visited the village, looking for shelter. Suryan was reluctant, but gave him a corner of the home. The sage observed that Suryan was still miserable, and said,' Your pain is not in the world outside—it is in your energy flow. Your heart is shut, your energy centers are closed.'

"Suryan, doubtful but desperate, replied, 'How do I heal what I can't see?'

"The sage smiled and replied, 'By stirring the jar of energy that is within you." Come, let me show you.'

"The sage taught him about chakras—these energy centers in our body controlling various facets of life. Then, over weeks, aided by breathwork, meditation and acts of love, Suryan began to heal. He learned that his pain, his anger and even his joy were all related to these energy centers. By straightening them, he found peace — not only with himself, but with the world around him."

Advait paused, allowing the story to sit. "The *chakras (energy centers)* are more than ancient mysticism — they're a map of the inside. Love in particular resides in the heart chakra, but it moves throughout all seven centers, each serving its own purpose."

The Seven Chakras And The Path Of Love

Advait pointed at the mandala on the floor. "The *chakras,* as mentioned in the *Vedic* and *Tantric* traditions, are like wheels of energy, spinning along your spine." He continued,"Let us examine them in the context of love."

Root Chakra (Muladhara): Foundation and Safety
Symbol: Red lotus.
Aspect of Love: Feeling grounded and safe allows you to love without fear.
Modern Relevance: In a fast-paced life, love often falters due to insecurity. Strengthening the root chakra helps

anchor relationships in stability.
Practice: Grounding through mindful walking—barefoot on grass or earth.

Sacral Chakra (Swadhisthana): Creativity and Sensuality
Symbol: Orange lotus.
Aspect of Love: This chakra governs pleasure and intimacy, allowing you to connect on a physical and creative level.
Modern Relevance: In a world that often suppresses genuine sensuality, balancing this chakra helps restore authentic connection.
Practice: Dance or movement meditation to free emotional and creative blocks.

Solar Plexus Chakra (Manipura): Power and Confidence
Symbol: Yellow lotus.
Aspect of Love: Confidence in oneself allows for healthy boundaries and mutual respect in love.
Modern Relevance: Balancing this chakra combats the ego-driven conflicts that arise in modern relationships.
Practice: Breath of fire (fast rhythmic breathing) to ignite personal power.

Heart Chakra (Anahata): Unconditional Love
Symbol: Green lotus.
Aspect of Love: The seat of love, compassion, and forgiveness.
Modern Relevance: In an age of transactional relationships, an open heart chakra fosters genuine connection.
Practice: Guided visualization (explained below) to align heart energy.

Throat Chakra (Vishuddha): Communication

Symbol: Blue lotus.
Aspect of Love: Honest communication builds trust and intimacy.
Modern Relevance: Miscommunication is a common pitfall in relationships. A balanced throat chakra encourages clarity and kindness.
Practice: Chanting or humming to release tension in the throat.

Third Eye Chakra (Ajna): Intuition
Symbol: Indigo lotus.
Aspect of Love: Seeing beyond words and actions into the essence of your partner.
Modern Relevance: Intuition allows deeper understanding amidst the chaos of modern life.
Practice: Candle-gazing meditation to enhance inner vision.

Crown Chakra (Sahasrara): Spiritual Connection
Symbol: Violet lotus.
Aspect of Love: Transcending personal love to experience universal love.
Modern Relevance: Connecting with the divine helps place everyday struggles in a greater perspective.
Practice: Silent meditation focusing on the top of the head.

Guided Visualization: Aligning The Heart Chakra

Advait invited Elina and Ishaan to close their eyes. "Let us practice aligning the heart chakra. This visualization will help you access the love within you and share it freely."

Preparation: Sit comfortably with your spine straight. Place your hands on your heart.

Step 1: Green Light Visualization
Inhale deeply, imagining a warm green light glowing in your chest.
With each exhale, picture this light expanding outward, enveloping your entire body.

Step 2: Connection to Others
Imagine the green light flowing from your heart to someone you love.
Send them forgiveness, gratitude, or compassion, whatever feels natural.

Step 3: Connection to Self
Now, turn the green light inward, letting it fill any spaces of self-doubt or pain.
Affirm to yourself, "I am love. I am enough."

Step 4: Universal Love
Finally, let the green light expand beyond you, connecting with the world, like ripples in a pond.

As the exercise ended, both Elina and Ishaan opened their eyes, their faces softened. "I felt... lighter," Elina said. "Like I wasn't just giving love—I was receiving it too."

"That is the essence of the heart chakra," Advait said. "It is not about taking or giving but about flow. *Love is not a possession; it is energy that moves through us.*"

Ancient Wisdom For Modern Life

Ishaan leaned forward, intrigued. "How does this apply to people like us—always busy, always moving?"

"Precisely because you are busy," Advait said, "this practice is essential. The fast pace of modern life blocks our energy centers with stress, fear, and distraction. When your chakras are aligned, you live with greater awareness and harmony. It takes just ten minutes a day to reconnect with yourself."

He added, "The sages knew this. As the *Yoga Sutras* teach,

'योगश्चित्तवृत्तिनिरोधः।'
(Yogaś citta-vṛtti-nirodhaḥ.)
('Yoga is the stilling of the fluctuations of the mind.')

The chakras are not just for ancient mystics—they are tools for anyone seeking balance in the chaos of life." Advait concluded.

That evening, as Elina and Ishaan practiced the guided visualization in their room, Elina placed her hand on Ishaan's chest.

"I can feel your heartbeat," she said softly. "It's strong."

"And steady," Ishaan replied. "Maybe that's what we've been missing—not just love, but balance."

Advait's words echoed in their minds: "*When the heart is open, love flows freely. When love flows freely, it awakens the soul.*"

The mandala of the chakras on the floor of the meditation hall seemed to glow faintly in the moonlight—a reminder that the path to love begins within.

∞∞∞

The Bridge of Words

The Power of Communication in Relationships

The air at *Antara* was sharp with morning when Ishaan and Elina walked to the retreat's open courtyard. Today felt different. After days of talking about vulnerability, intimacy and energy, they both discovered that beneath their struggles was a deeper issue: *how they communicated with each other?* They were interested, but hesitant, to try this part of them out.

As was his habit, Advait greeted them with calmness. In the middle was a small round table with a notebook and two clay cups of herbal tea.

Today," he started, "we get into the bridge of the souls: commuunication —" When done mindfully, it connects; when done carelessly, it divides."

The Couple And The Silent Monk

Then Advait started by narrating a tale of the couple and the silent monk, "Once upon a time, in a busy contemporary city, there lived a couple named Aryan and Meera. Aryan was a tech entrepreneur, always busy doing work. Aryan is working for their future, and Meera, a teacher, has no reason to feel neglected. Every evening ended with a fight — Meera attacking his loneliness, Aryan, hers.

"One weekend, they went to a silent retreat led by a monk who never spoke. There was one rule of the retreat: The participants couldn't talk with one another except by writing notes.

"Aryan and Meera had a hard time at first. Meera's notes were lengthy and impassioned; Aryan's were terse and combative. But by the end of the weekend, something had changed. Without the din of their voices, they started decoding and contemplating each other's words. Meera felt how much Aryan craved intimacy, and Aryan understood the weight Meera bore. By the end of the retreat they had written a note that just said 'I see you. I hear you. Let's try again.'

"The monk who had listened to them silently finally uttered a sentence and said: '*True communication starts when the noise ends.*' "

The Three Pillars Of Conscious Communication

Advait set down his tea cup. "The story of Aryan and Meera demonstrates that communication is not just about words alone—it is the presence, the intention and the understanding. Conscious communication has three pillars."

1. Listening Without Reacting

"Most of us listen to respond, not to understand. This creates a cycle of defensiveness," Advait explained. "To truly listen, you must quiet your inner dialogue and give your full attention to the other person."

Practice: Active Listening Exercise

Choose a Time: Set aside 10 minutes daily to have an uninterrupted conversation.

One Speaks, One Listens: The speaker shares their thoughts without interruption, while the listener only nods or makes affirming sounds.

Reflect Back: The listener paraphrases what they heard: "What I hear you saying is..."

Switch Roles: Reverse the roles to ensure both feel heard.

Relevance in a Fast-Paced Life: This practice can be done during dinner or even while driving together. The key is intention, not perfection.

2. Speaking With Intention

Advait continued, "Words have power. The *Upanishads* teach us,

'वाणीं सदा सत्यं वदेत्।'
(Vāṇīṁ sadā satyaṁ vadet.)
('Speak only that which is true and kind.')

"When we speak with awareness, our words become tools for connection, not weapons for division."

Practice: The Pause Before Speaking

Pause: Before speaking in a charged moment, take a deep breath.

Ask Yourself: Is it true? Is it necessary? Is it kind?

Speak Clearly: Use "I" statements to express feelings. For example, instead of "You never listen," say, "I feel unheard when I share something important."

Relevance in a Fast-Paced Life: This can be incorporated into everyday disagreements or work discussions. The pause takes seconds but transforms the tone of communication.

3. Resolving Conflicts With Compassion

"Conflict is inevitable," Advait said, "but it doesn't have to be destructive. In Nonviolent Communication (NVC), we learn to separate observation from judgment and express needs without blame."

Practice: The Four Steps of NVC

Observation: Describe the situation without adding judgment.

Instead of: "You're always late," say: "I noticed you arrived 20 minutes later than we planned."

Feelings: Share how it makes you feel.
"I felt frustrated because..."

Needs: Express your unmet need.
"I need reliability to feel secure."

Request: Make a clear, actionable request.
"Could you let me know if you'll be late next time?"

Relevance in a Fast-Paced Life: Even in text messages or quick exchanges, this framework can defuse tension and build understanding.

Practical Ritual: The "Listening Bowl"

That evening, Advait suggested a private ritual to Ishaan and Elina to deepen their communication.

The Ritual: The Listening Bowl

Preparation: Place a bowl on the table between you and write down one question or topic each person wants to discuss.
Step 1: Set the Space: Light a candle and agree to take turns speaking and listening without interruptions.

Step 2: Use a Symbol: Hold a small object, such as a stone, to signify the speaker's turn. Only the person holding the object speaks.

Step 3: Reflect: After each person speaks, the listener reflects back what they heard before responding.

Step 4: Close: End the ritual with a shared affirmation, such as, "Thank you for sharing. I value your voice."

Elina and Ishaan found the practice surprisingly powerful.

"It forced us to slow down," Ishaan admitted. "I realized how often I cut Elina off without meaning to."

Elina added, "And I realized I sometimes assume Ishaan isn't listening when he actually is."

Communication As Energy

"The sages believed," Advait said, "that *communication is an exchange of energy, not just words. When you listen mindfully, you give your partner the gift of presence. When you speak intentionally, you create a bridge of understanding.*"

He recited a verse from the *Yoga Sutras*:

"सत्यं चितं आनंदं वाणीं।"
(Satyaṁ cittaṁ ānandaṁ vāṇīṁ.)
('Truth, awareness, and joy flow through mindful speech.')

As they left the pavilion, Advait gave them one final suggestion: "Tonight, practice listening—not just to each other, but to the silence between your words. Sometimes, the most profound truths are found in the spaces we often overlook."

That evening, as they sat with the listening bowl, Ishaan said, "I didn't realize how much noise I bring to our conversations."

"And I didn't realize how much I hold back," Elina replied. "Maybe it's not about saying more, but about saying it better."

The flame of their candle flickered gently, illuminating the quiet smiles on their faces—a reminder that in the stillness of understanding, love finds its voice.

∞∞∞

Rituals of Love

Sacred Practices to Deepen Connection

The sun had set and the sky above *Antara* was aflame with orange and purple. It was as if the air emanating from the retreat was alive; as if every breath brought with it possibilities. Advait was waiting for Ishaan and Elina in the candlelit meditation hall. Tonight's session felt different — more intimate, more profound.

"Connection," Advait started, his words echoing in the silence, "is not an accident. It is worked, like a holy garden. Tonight we when we think of rituals — not obligations — but ways to cultivate love."

Once There Was A Master Of *Tao*

Advait relaxed into a meditative pose and told a story. "Xian, a venerated master, resided in a small Taoist village high up in the mountains of ancient China. He was wise, and he brought together everyone and everything who respectfully needed him.

"One day, a couple came to Xian. They had been together for a long time, but they were growing apart. The husband began: 'Master, we no longer understand each other. Something that used to feel easy now feels like a weight.'

The master listened and replied: "*Love, like water, must flow. When it stops flowing, it is a swamp. When it flows, it nourishes.* I am going to show you a very easy ritual.'

"He took them to a stream and gave each a little bowl. 'Every morning,' he said, 'fill these bowls with water from the stream and present them to each other and say, "I give you my presence and I give you my love." In the evening, tip the water back into the stream while saying, "I release all grievances and renew our bond." '

"The couple followed the advice of the Xian with utmost sincerity. Gradually, their mornings became sacred, their evenings rejuvenating. In this ritual, they found their love's flow again."

Advait looked at Ishaan and Elina. "*Rituals, when practiced intentionally, create sacred moments of connection. They remind us of the good stuff in life, even when life gets busy.*"

The Philosophy Of Deeper Rituals

"Rituals are ancient tools for grounding and connection," Advait said. "In Hindu, Buddhist, and Taoist traditions, rituals are more than ceremonies — they are portals to presence and intention."

He quoted the *Bhagavad Gita*:

"योग: कर्मसु कौशलम्।"
(Yogaḥ karmasu kauśalam.)
"'Yoga is skill in action.' A ritual is a skillful action, one that transforms the mundane into the sacred."

"Modern life is fast-paced, but rituals are a kind of anchor," Advait explained. They make room for love to breathe, even when everything seems chaotic. A ritual does not require an elaborate plan; it requires just two elements: intention and attention."

Practical Rituals For Connection

Advait leaned forward, speaking almost conversationally. "Let me share three simple rituals that you can do daily that will deepen your connection."

1. The Morning Offering

Purpose: Begin the day with gratitude and presence.

Practice: (a) Sit together for five minutes in the morning, (b) Light a small candle and say aloud, "I offer you my love, my presence, and my gratitude.", and (c) If apart, send this as a text or silently affirm it during your morning meditation.

Modern Relevance: This ritual can be done quickly but sets a tone of connection for the day.

2. The Evening Release

Purpose: Let go of grievances and renew your bond.

Practice: (a) Before bed, hold each other's hands and take three deep breaths together, (b) Share one thing you appreciated about each other that day, (c) If there was conflict, say, "I release this with love and begin a new."

Modern Relevance: A few minutes each night can heal small fractures before they become divides.

3. The Weekly Sacred Meal

Purpose: Dedicate time to mindful presence and nourishment.
Practice: (a) Choose one meal a week to eat together in silence, focusing on the food and each other's presence,

and (b) Begin the meal by saying, "May this nourish our bodies and our connection."

Modern Relevance: Even a busy schedule can accommodate one sacred meal, turning an everyday activity into a bonding experience.

The Circle Of Connection (Private Ritual)

That evening, Advait introduced Ishaan and Elina to a private ritual they could perform in their room.

The Ritual: The Circle of Connection

Preparation: (a) Sit facing each other with a small bowl of water between you, and (b) Light a candle and dim the room's lights to create a calm atmosphere.

Step 1: Opening the Circle: (a) Each partner places a hand on the bowl., (b) Say together: "This circle is sacred. Within it, we are safe, seen, and loved."

Step 2: Sharing Intentions: Take turns sharing one intention for the relationship, beginning with "I intend to..." (e.g., "I intend to listen more deeply.")

Step 3: Sealing the Connection: (a) Dip your fingers into the water and touch your partner's forehead or hands., and (b) Say, "I honor you and our bond."

Step 4: Closing the Circle: Blow out the candle together and sit in silence for a moment, holding hands.

Elina found herself tearing up during the ritual.

"It felt... grounding," she said afterward. "Like we were creating something bigger than ourselves."

"It was more intimate than any conversation we've had," Ishaan added. "It made me realize how often I take our connection for granted."

The Relevance Of Rituals In Modern Life

As they shared their experience with Advait the next morning, Ishaan asked, "How do we make time for these rituals with everything else going on in life?"

"Rituals don't require hours," Advait replied. "They require presence. Even in the busiest day, a moment of intention can change the energy of your relationship. A ritual is not about time—it is about attention."

He quoted from the *Tao Te Ching*:

"Do you have the patience to wait till your mud settles and the water is clear?"

"Rituals," he explained, "are how we let the mud of life settle, revealing the clarity of love."

Create Your Own Rituals

Advait concluded, "The rituals I've shared are guides, but the most powerful rituals are the ones you create together. Ask yourselves: What small act can we do daily, weekly, or monthly to honor our connection?"

As Ishaan and Elina walked through the gardens that evening, they began brainstorming their own rituals.

"What if we start writing each other little notes again?" Elina suggested.

“And maybe share a quick hug every morning before the chaos starts,” Ishaan added.

The moonlight bathed *Antara* in a gentle glow, mirroring the quiet sense of renewal between them. In their hearts, they knew: *Rituals weren’t just practices—they were promises, kept and renewed with love.*

∞∞∞

Self-Love

The Building Block of Any Connection

The low afternoon sun saturated *Antara* with warmth and golden hues as Ishaan and Elina strolled towards the library. Today's session seemed heavy with anticipation. In the past few days they had examined their relationship, worked toward better communication, practiced rituals to help each other feel loved. But now, Advait had suggested something more profound — a quest to return to self.

When they entered, Advait was sitting by the window, looking out at the canopy of trees. Only one mirror lay on the table next to him, its glass gleaming. He turned to face them, his expression placid but solemn.

"Today, we examine a truth that many averse to, yet all must accept," Advait said. *"Self-love is the basis for any connection.* Without love, your love for others is incomplete. Without it, your relationships don't blossom."

Tara: A Journey To Self-Acceptance

Advait began with a story. "There was a young woman named Tara, who hails from a small town in India. Tara was kind, smart and beautiful, but she had this deep wound, this feeling that she was never enough. Despite everything she achieved, Tara didn't feel worthy of love and acceptance.

"Tara sought approval from others for years, thinking approval from outside would mend her." She found herself in relationships where she was all in, but always came up flat. With every failed relationship, her insecurity grew deeper, leading her to conclude that there was something wrong with her.

"One day, Tara was walking on the street when she met an old artist who lived in her town. He was famous for designing beautiful mirrors that wasn't just a reflection of a face but, as legend said, the soul. Tara was curious, and went to see his studio.

"The artist gave her a mirror and said, 'Look carefully. What do you see?'

"She looked at herself in the mirror and started to enumerate the flaws. Her uneven skin, her too-wide smile, her sleepy eyes.

"The artist smiled and said, 'What you see is not the mirror's reflection — it is your own judgment. This mirror is truthful, but it presents only what you decide to perceive. Can you look again, but this time with love?'"

"Tara hesitated but tried. Gradually, she started to view herself differently. Her eyes were weary, sure, but they were also shall we say: kind. Her smile was broad, but warm and inviting. As days grew into weeks, Tara increasingly visited the artist, where she learned to look at herself with kindness. Over time her relationships started to shift — not because people treated her differently, but because she treated herself differently.

"The artist's parting words to her were, '*When you love yourself, you teach others how to love you. You become the reflection of the love you want to get.*' "

Advait looked at Ishaan and Elina with his trademark calm smile and continued. "Tara's story reminds us that *the love we seek will always start inside of us. Without self-love, every relationship we have is on shaky ground.*"

The Philosophy Of Self-Love

Advait added, "OSHO talks about self-love as not being selfish but the beginning of wholeness. According to OSHO,

> *Unless you love yourself, you cannot love anybody else. You will always be afraid of losing the other, because the other becomes your source of love.'*

When you love yourself, you no longer seek completion in others—you share your completeness."

He quoted a verse from the *Bhagavad Gita*:

"आत्मानं विद्धि, आत्मप्रेमं विद्धि।"
(Ātmānaṁ viddhi, ātmapremaṁ viddhi.)
('Know thyself, and in knowing, love thyself.')

Why Self-Love Matters In Modern Life?

Elina raised a question. "But how do we be kind to ourselves in a world that tells us we're not good enough? Social media, work pressure — it's all contributing to this feeling of always not measuring up."

Advait nodded. "Modern life does beat up on self-doubt. But the very speed of life that makes self-love difficult also makes it necessary. *By focusing on self-love, you build a sanctuary within yourself; a place no one can touch."*

"Self-love is not indulgence," he added. "It is discipline. It is not about indulging yourself but about recognizing your needs, maintaining boundaries and speaking to yourself in a kind way."

Practical Techniques For Cultivating Self-Love

Advait looked at Ishaan and Elina in a clam yet determined manner, and said, "Let me share few practices with you that will help you to cultivate self-love."

1. Mirror Meditation

Purpose: To confront and accept yourself as you are.

Practice: (a) Sit in front of a mirror in a quiet space, (b) Look into your own eyes and hold your gaze. At first, this may feel uncomfortable, but stay with it., (c) Say aloud, "I see you. I accept you. I love you.", and (d) Repeat this daily, observing how your feelings toward yourself evolve.

Relevance in Modern Life: This practice requires only five minutes but builds a foundation of self-acceptance over time.

2. The Compassion Journal

Purpose: To shift your internal narrative from criticism to compassion.

Practice: (a) Each evening, write down three things you appreciate about yourself. These can be qualities, actions, or even small victories., (b) When you notice self-critical thoughts during the day, pause and reframe them: Instead of "I failed at this," say, "I am learning from this."

Relevance in Modern Life: This practice turns moments of self-doubt into opportunities for self-growth.

3. A Ritual for Self-Honor

Purpose: To create a physical act of self-love.

Practice: (a) Light a candle and sit in silence., (b) Place your hand on your heart and repeat the affirmation: "I am worthy of love, exactly as I am.", (c) Write yourself a letter, expressing gratitude for your strengths and compassion for your struggles., and (d) Read the letter aloud to yourself, as though speaking to a dear friend.

Relevance in Modern Life: This ritual can be done weekly, creating a sacred space to reconnect with yourself.

The Circle Of Self-Love (Individual Private Practice)

That evening, Advait suggested a private ritual called "*The Circile of Self-Love*" for Elina and Ishaan to practice individually.

Preparation: (a) Sit in a quiet space with a small bowl of water and a flower., and (b) Light a candle to create a calming atmosphere.

Step 1: Reflection: Look into the water and speak aloud one thing you forgive yourself for.

Step 2: Gratitude: Place the flower in the water and say, "I honor myself for [name a quality or action]."

Step 3: Affirmation: Touch your heart and repeat: "I am enough. I am whole. I am loved."

Step 4: Release: Pour the water into a plant or onto the earth, symbolizing renewal.

Self-Love Is A Practice

The next morning, as Ishaan and Elina shared their experiences, Advait said, "*Self-love is not a destination—it is a practice.* It is the well from which all other love flows. When you love yourself, you do not fear loss, for you carry love within you."

He recited a verse from the *Vigyan Bhairav Tantra*:

"स्वं स्वं मनोवृत्तिं चित्तं, शिवं परं प्रकाशते।"
(Svaṁ svaṁ manovṛttiṁ cittaṁ, śivaṁ paraṁ prakāśate.)
('When the mind rests in its own essence, it reflects the divine light within.')

As they walked back to their room, Elina turned to Ishaan. "This isn't just about us, is it? It's about finding ourselves."

Ishaan nodded. "And maybe, when we do, everything else will fall into place."

The mirror in the library, still gleaming in the morning light, seemed to echo the quiet truth of the day: love begins with the self.

∞∞∞

The Healing Power of Love

From Hurt to Harmony Through Compassion

The air on *Antara* was oddly quiet, as if the wood itself was holding its breath. Indulging & immersed in conversations, Ishaan & Elina sat under the banyan tree, Advait awaited there. His brow furrowed, his usual serenity touched with a remote gravity. "Today" he began "we speak of one of love's greatest powers — its ability to heal — not just people but nations";

He looked from one to the other, his voice tender but firm. "*Healing through love demands that we rise above hurt, above resentment, and toward compassion.* Let me tell you a story of someone who did,"

The Story Of The War Survivor

"In a village marred by war," Advait began, "there was a man named Daya. He had lost everything: his home, his family, even his sense of purpose. The war had ended; Daya's fight continued. He found himself full of rage and resentment toward the solders who had ruined this life.

"One day a monk came to the village. He was this monk who was radiating this serene energy, not perturbed at all by the visible devastation and destruction around him.

Daya was curious about monk's composure. Daya followed the monk and asked him, 'How could you keep so much peace while seeing so much destruction? How do you not hate the people who did this?'

"The monk said, 'Hatred is like to take a burning coal in your hand with an intention to throw it to another. Who gets burned first?'

"Daya made a face but didn't say anything. The monk said, '*Healing does not come through vengeance. It comes from compassion.* Let me tell you about *Karuna*—compassion for all beings, even those who hurt us.

"In the ensuing weeks, the monk introduced Daya to meditative practices and small acts of kindness. He asked Daya to plant trees in the village as a sign of rebirth. Gradually Daya's anger began to soften. Instead of feeling like a victim, he felt like a healer.

"Years passed, and the trees Daya had planted blossomed into a verdant grove where the villagers would come often to mediate and make peace with one another. And Daya came to be known not for how he suffered but for how he loved — a reflection of love's redemptive nature.

Advait paused for the story to set. "Daya was not the only one who changed. Its ripple effect extended to everyone in his village. This is the essence of *Karuna* — compassion which goes beyond individual pain and creates healing together."

Healing With Love: The Philosophy

Advait turned to the couple. "Compassion is at the heart of many ancient teachings. In Buddhism, it is known as *Karuna*. Compassion is not pity, the Buddha taught —

it is the active desire (self initiated efforts) to relieve the suffering of others. But true compassion begins with ourselves."

He quoted from the *Dhammapada*:

"न हि वेरेन वेरानि, सम्मन्ति इध कुदाचनं।
अवेरेन च सम्मन्ति, एस धम्मो सनन्तनो।"
(Na hi verena verāni, sammantī idha kudācanaṁ.
Averena ca sammantī, esa dhammo sanantano.)
('Hatred does not cease by hatred. It ceases
only by love. This is an eternal truth.')

He went on, "OSHO often spoke of compassion as love in action. He said, '*When you are compassionate, you are no longer an individual. You are a vast energy that embraces all existence.*' This energy has the power to heal wounds that logic or time alone cannot."

Techniques For Cultivating Compassion

Advait suggested a series of practices to Ishaan and Elina to internalise compassion in their lives.

1. The Loving-Kindness Meditation (*Metta Bhavana*)

Purpose: To develop compassion for yourself and others.

Practice: (a) Sit in a comfortable position and close your eyes, (b) Begin by silently repeating: "May I be happy. May I be healthy. May I be free from suffering.", (c) Gradually extend this wish to others: first to loved ones, then to neutral people, and finally to those you find difficult., and (d) End with: "May all beings everywhere be happy and free from suffering."

Relevance in Modern Life: This meditation can be

practiced for just five minutes a day, even during a commute or before bed.

2. The Ritual of Forgiveness

Purpose: To release anger and make space for healing.

Practice: (a) Write down the name of someone who has hurt you, (b) On one side of the paper, write how their actions affected you. On the other side, write, "I release this pain. I forgive you and set myself free.", (c) Burn the paper safely, symbolizing release.

Relevance in Modern Life: This ritual can be performed whenever resentment builds, offering immediate emotional relief.

3. Acts of Compassion

Purpose: To make compassion a daily habit.

Practice: (a) Each day, perform one act of kindness —smiling at a stranger, helping a colleague, or volunteering., and (b) Reflect on how these actions make you feel, reinforcing the cycle of compassion.

Relevance in Modern Life: Small, intentional acts of kindness can be seamlessly integrated into busy schedules.

Advait suggested a private ritual for Elina and Ishaan to perform that evening.

The Compassion Bowl (Private Ritual)

Preparation: (a) Fill a bowl with water and place it between you., (b) Light a candle to create a calm, sacred space.

Step 1: Naming the Hurt: Take turns sharing something

that has caused pain or resentment, whether in your relationship or elsewhere. Speak without blaming.

Step 2: Offering Compassion: For each hurt shared, the other responds, "I see your pain, and I offer you compassion."

Step 3: Releasing the Pain: Together, pour the water into the earth outside, symbolizing the release of shared burdens.

Step 4: Closing the Ritual: End by placing a hand on each other's hearts and repeating: "We choose love. We choose compassion."

Elina felt a sense of lightness after the ritual. "It was hard to share those feelings, but it also felt... freeing."

Ishaan nodded. "And it made me realize how often I overlook your pain while focusing on my own."

Advait's Reflection

Later that evening, when the couple shared their experience with Advait he reflected. "The greatest gift you can give is your compassion. It heals not just others, but yourself. Compassion is the bridge that transforms pain into love, resentment into forgiveness."

He recited a verse from the *Vigyan Bhairav Tantra*:

"दया सर्वभूतानां, हृदयस्य श्रेष्ठमं तत्त्वम्।"
(Dayā sarvabhūtānāṁ, hṛdayasya śreṣṭhamaṁ tattvam.)
('Compassion for all beings is the highest truth of the heart.')

Advait added, "When you practice compassion, you transcend the small self. You become a vessel for healing, not just for yourself, but for the world."

As Elina and Ishaan walked back to their room, the quiet of the evening mirrored their own introspection.

"Compassion isn't just about others," Elina said. "It's about setting ourselves free."

"And it's not always easy," Ishaan added. "But maybe that's where its power lies—in choosing love when it's hardest."

The trees of *Antara* stood tall and silent, their roots intertwined beneath the earth—a quiet reminder that even amidst pain, there is always room for growth and connection.

∞∞∞

Love and Creativity

Fueling the Inner Flame

The atmosphere at *Antara* was electric, crackling with the energy of mid-morning sun streaming through trees. Elina and Ishaan went into the art studio — a calm space they hadn't visited before. It was covered in paintings, sculptures, and various types of mandalas, all textured and seeming alive.

Advait was waiting, next to an unfinished painting of a lotus emerging at the center of spiraling cosmic waves. "Welcome," he said, waving at the art surrounding them. "Today we dive into the relationship between love and creativity — two forces that, when put together, can bring about a reinvention of your inner world."

He put his hand on the painting in front of him. "Love is not only an emotion. Energy is what it is; creativity is how you express it. And I'd like to tell you a story about an artist who figured this out."

Tale Of The Inspiration By The Divine Feminine

"In a small coastal town, Advait said, there lived an artist called Amara. Her paintings were known for their vibrant colors and emotional intensity. But for years, Amara felt separated from her art. She painted in the same way, churning out works that sold but never satisfied her.

“One day, Amara went to an old temple dedicated to the *Goddess Durga*, the personification of the divine feminine. When the temple priestess saw Amara’s troubled face, she said, ‘The Goddess gives freely, but only to those who approach her with an open heart. Why do you carry this burden?’

“Amara paused before admitting, ‘I feel empty, as if the spark that once ignited my art has been extinguished.’

“The priestess gave her a little clay lamp and said, ‘Light this in front of the Goddess and offer to her your emptiness. She will pour you full of what you seek.”

“Amara did as instructed. As she sat in the temple's glow, she felt a shift within her. Instead of emptiness within her, a space was being formed to embrace something new and creative. She began to see love not as something to possess but as an energy that could flow into her art, her life, and her relationships.

“From that day on, Amara’s paintings changed. No more was she painting to impress; now she painted from a bottomless well of love that she had hidden deep within herself. Her work became a meditation, a prayer, a celebration of the divine feminine.”

Advait smiled. “Amara’s story reminds us that *the essence of creativity is love*. When we open ourselves up to love — not just romantic love but universal love — it burns the fuel of expression.”

The Philosophy Of Love And Creativity

“Creativity,” Advait added, “is not just art. It is a way of being. It is how you see the world, tackle challenges, care for connections, and communicate with your essence. Love is the gas that runs this creativity."

He quoted OSHO:

"Creativity is the fragrance of real freedom. When you love deeply, you are free, and in that freedom, creativity blooms.'

He also cited the *Rigveda*, which depicts creation as the act of a loving god:

"कामस्य कमा यदजायन्त विश्वे।"
(Kāmasya kamā yadajāyanta viśve.)
('From love arose the desire to create, and thus the universe was born.')

"The sages knew love and creativity go hand in hand," Advait said. The more deeply you love — yourself, other people, the divine — the more you unleash the creative force."

The Role Of Creativity In Modern Life

Elina raised a question. "But in the world we live in now, how do you cultivate creativity when you have work commitments and responsibilities?"

"Exactly because life is so fast," Advait replied, "creativity is very important. It's not a luxury; it's how you tap back into yourself amidst that chaos. Creativity is the bridge back to your essence."

He added: "Modern creativity doesn't have to do with painting or composing symphonies. It could be as straightforward as making a meal with love, writing a letter — "anything that's infused with your meaning, or if you're wanting it to be about life, or wanting to bring force, or love, or energy" — or it could be something more ambitious like a "re-imagining of how you work."

Practices To Expand Creativity With Love

Advait used these insights to introduce some practices that would help Elina and Ishaan tap into their creative energy.

1. Creative Journaling for Emotional Expression

Purpose: To transform emotions into inspiration.

Practice: (a) Set aside 10–15 minutes in a quiet space., (b) Write freely about your feelings, whether joyful or painful, without judgment., (c) Use prompts like "What does love feel like today?" or "What am I longing to express?", and (d) Conclude with a sentence of gratitude for the process.

Relevance in Modern Life: Journaling is a flexible practice that can be done anytime, offering emotional clarity and creative insight.

2. The Sacred Gesture

Purpose: To connect physical movement with creative energy.

Practice: (a) Stand in an open space and close your eyes., (b) Imagine a golden light at your heart center, representing love., (c) Begin moving your arms gently, letting the light flow through your movements., and (d) Allow your body to guide you, creating gestures that feel natural and expressive.

Relevance in Modern Life: This practice takes just a few minutes and can be a quick reset during a busy day.

3. The Creativity Altar

Purpose: To create a physical space for inspiration.

Practice: (a) Choose a small area in your home and dedicate it to creativity., (b) Place objects that inspire you—photos, quotes, or items from nature., and (c) Spend a few minutes daily at the altar, reflecting or creating.

Relevance in Modern Life: The altar serves as a visual reminder to prioritize creative expression.

The Flame Of Creativity (Private Practice)

That evening, Advait suggested a private ritual for Elina and Ishaan to perform individually.

Preparation: (a) Light a candle and sit in front of it with a blank page or sketchbook.

Step 1: Reflection: Gaze into the flame and visualize it as the fire of love and inspiration within you.

Step 2: Expression: Begin to write, draw, or doodle freely, letting the flame guide your thoughts and emotions.

Step 3: Gratitude: Close the ritual by expressing gratitude for the creative energy that flows through you.

Step 4: Sharing (Optional): If comfortable, share your creation with your partner or keep it as a personal expression.

Elina found herself sketching abstract shapes that reflected her emotions, while Ishaan wrote a short, heartfelt note to Elina, something he hadn't done in years. Both felt a renewed sense of connection—not just to each other, but to themselves.

Creativity As Love In Action

The next morning, Advait shared a final thought. “Creativity is not about perfection. It is about expression. It is love in action—a way to honor the divine within you.”

He recited a verse from the *Tao Te Ching*:

"The heart that loves creates effortlessly, for it flows with the rhythm of life."

He added, “When you allow love to fuel your creativity, you are not just creating art—you are creating a more meaningful life.”

As Elina and Ishaan walked back through the gardens, Ishaan said, “I never thought of creativity as something I could practice daily. But it feels... liberating.”

Elina smiled. “It’s like we’re learning to express parts of ourselves we’ve kept hidden.”

The lotus blooms in the studio reflected their own journey—each petal a layer of love and creativity, unfolding toward the light.

∞∞∞

Love Transcended

From Physical Union to Cosmic Unity

The sun hung low over the retreat at *Antara*, casting long shadows over the banyan tree. As Ishaan and Elina entered the open meditation pavilion for their last evening together, the air was thick with expectancy. Over the last few days they had peeled back layers of their relationship, explored their vulnerabilities, and taken on new practices of love and connection. Tonight, Advait's demeanor was changed — his piling-mountain lightness now filled with a silent awe.

"Tonight," Advait began, "we walk beyond the personal, beyond the physical, into the universal. Because love, when fully realized, leaves behind the barriers of self and other. It melts away the illusion of separateness and brings us to cosmic unity."

Elina turned her head and thought for a moment. "Cosmic unity?"

Advait nodded. "Yes. Let me share a story."

An Unlikely Friendship

"There once lived a mystic called Arav on the mountains far away from the clatter of the world. People flocked to him to ask for advice, hearing legends of his deep sagacity."

“And one day, a couple went to see him. They were hopelessly in love but felt like they were constrained by words, emotions, even closeness. ‘We feel close,’ the woman said, ‘but not all there.’ We desire to transcend what we have experienced.’

Arav listened patiently and replied, “Come with me." He guided them to a clearing beneath a wide, starlit sky. He sat with them: "Close your eyes and breathe. Sense the rhythm of breath, the beating of heart. Now release your names, your titles, even your bodies. Imagine that you are one, not two."

“The couple struggled at the beginning. And their minds were clinging to their identities, their identities as husband and wife. But after a time, under Arav’s cue, they began to melt into the moment. They could sense the cool earth beneath, the great stretch of sky above, the heartbeat of the universe inside.

“When they opened their eyes, they were different.” They had blurred into each other. Their minds opened to the realization that their love was not just between the two of them — it was a manifestation of the universal love that needs to pulse through all things.

Arav smiled and said, ‘You have reached the depth of love. It is not yours or mine. It is the fundamental fabric of existence itself.’ ”

Advait paused, allowing the story to sink in. “This is a love transcended journey. It starts with two, but it ends in oneness — with one another, with the universe.”

Love Is Transcendence

"OSHO spoke about love as a gateway to transcendence more than anything," Advait continued. He said,

'Love is when two souls meet. "But the greatest love is when you and that other soul dissolve in the infinite, the divine.'

But love that is beyond the personal is universal. It's not about having or being had anymore. It's about merging with the greater whole."

He quoted a verse from the *Bhagavad Gita*:

"मम आत्मा सर्वभूतात्मा, योगयुक्तो भवेति च।"
(Mama ātmā sarvabhūtātmā, yogayukto bhaveti ca.)
('My soul is the soul of all beings, united through yoga.')

"This is the essence of *Tantra*," Advait added — "the union of opposites, the merging of dualities, the dissolution of ego into the infinite."

From Physical Love To Cosmic Love

Ishaan raised a question. "But how do we transition from the physical to the cosmic? It feels... abstract."

Know this, Advait answered: "The physical isn't apart from the cosmic. The body is a portal, not a prison. Tantra teaches us that the physical is sacred and should be honored, but must be used to transcend."

He sketched a simple diagram on the sand — a small circle within a larger circle. "The little circle is your personal love, your couple. The bigger circle is universal love that is connection to all existence. To quote my fellow realist, Jill Lepore, "*The path from one to the other is not a path that rejects the physical but one that extends it.*"

Practical Techniques To Experience Cosmic Unity

They remained with Advait, who led practices that serve to lead the personal to bridge the universal.

1. The Breath of Unity

Purpose: To dissolve the boundaries of self and other.

Practice: (a) Sit facing each other and synchronize your breath., (b) Imagine that with each inhale, you draw in your partner's energy. With each exhale, you share your own., and (c) Gradually, expand your awareness beyond your partner, visualizing your breath connecting to the trees, the earth, and the stars.

Relevance in Modern Life: This practice can be done in moments of quiet, offering a sense of connection even amidst daily chaos.

2. The Cosmic Heart Meditation

Purpose: To experience love as a universal force.

Practice: (a) Sit comfortably with your eyes closed., (b) Place your hands on your heart and visualize a golden light radiating outward., (c) As the light expands, imagine it touching every being—family, friends, strangers, even those you find difficult to love., (d) End by affirming, "I am love. I am one with all that is."

Relevance in Modern Life: This meditation requires only a few minutes but fosters a profound sense of connection.

3. The Silent Union

Purpose: To connect without words or actions.

Practice: (a) Spend 10 minutes sitting back-to-back with your partner, focusing only on the shared energy between you., and (b) Imagine your energies merging and flowing as one.

Relevance in Modern Life: This practice is a powerful way to reconnect after a busy day.

The Night Under The Stars (Private Practice)

That evening, Advait suggested a ritual for Elina and Ishaan to perform in the open air.

Preparation: Find a quiet, open space under the night sky.
Lie down on a blanket, holding hands.

Step 1: Dissolving Boundaries: Focus on your breath and let your thoughts dissolve into the vastness of the stars above.

Step 2: Expanding Awareness: Imagine the boundaries of your body fading, merging with your partner, the earth, and the cosmos.

Step 3: Silent Connection: Spend 15 minutes in silence, simply being present with the universe.

Step 4: Closing Affirmation: End by whispering to each other, "We are one with all that is."

As they completed the ritual, Ishaan felt a deep stillness within. "It was like... I wasn't just me," he said. "I was everything."

Elina nodded, her eyes glistening. "I felt it too. It was like love wasn't just between us—it was everywhere."

Becoming The Universe

The next morning, Advait shared his final reflection on the session. "Love begins with the self, grows in relationship, and ultimately dissolves into the universal. This is its true purpose—not to bind, but to free."

He recited a verse from the *Vigyan Bhairav Tantra*:

"निर्वाणं यत्र प्रेमं, तत्र मोक्षं।"
(Nirvāṇaṁ yatra premaṁ, tatra mokṣaṁ.)
('Where love becomes liberation, there lies freedom.')

He added, "When you experience love as cosmic unity, you no longer fear loss or separation. You realize that love is the essence of existence itself."

As they walked back to their room, Ishaan and Elina felt a quiet peace between them.

"This isn't just about us, is it?" Elina said. "It's about something much bigger."

Ishaan nodded. "And maybe that's the point. Love isn't something we have. It's something we are."

Above them, the stars still lingered faintly in the morning sky—a quiet reminder that love, when transcended, is not bound by time, space, or form.

∞∞∞

The Art of Living Love

Bringing Love into Daily Life, Work, and Family

The early light of dawn broke through the trees at *Antara* as Ishaan and Elina walked towards the meditation pavilion. The air was fresh, with a hint of jasmine. It was the last of their guided sessions with Advait today, and both were filled with a sense of gratitude and anticipation. Over their time retreating, they had delved into the depths of love—its vulnerabilities, its spiritual dimensions, and its transformative power. But as they got ready to leave, a new question hung in the air: How do we take this knowledge back to our daily lives?

Advait sat alone in the pavilion, framed by the morning's silence. A small clay lamp burned beside him dipped in the breeze.

"Good morning," he said with a friendly smile. "Today, we complete our journey." We have looked at love as a state of being, and a force that transcends the physical, and the doorway to the divine. But *love also must be lived — distributed through the quotidian moments of life*."

How Do We Keep Love Alive?

"First, Elina, her voice concerned. "I've learned a lot here, but the world outside is so different. There are deadlines and responsibilities and distractions... How do we sustain this when we leave?"

Advait nodded thoughtfully. "This is a common challenge. Everyone else thinks love is only found in special moments — romantic dinners, spiritual retreats, grand gestures. Yet love isn't limited to occasions. It's a way of being, a way of looking at the world."

He pointed to the clay lamp next to him. "Think of this flame. It burns as flames feed on oil, shielded from the wind. Similarly, conscious love needs to be nurtured and cared for on a daily basis."

"He and "Integrating love into your life" refers to showing up with presence and purpose in your communications. Whether you're responding to an email, preparing a meal or playing with your child, consider: Am I doing this with love? That answer will change the act."

Can Love Flourish In A Competitive World?

Ishaan asked a question of his own. "In the world I inhabit, competition is everything. How do you balance love with ambition?"

"Uh-huh," Advait said, leaning a bit closer. "This is a fundamental misapprehension about love — and ambition." True ambition, though, isn't a matter of putting other people down — it is about raising yourself up. And love is not a weakness; it is that strength that allows you to grow without fear."

He was quoting, he said, from the *Bhagavad Gita*:

"कर्मण्येवाधिकारस्ते, मा फलेषु कदाचन।"

(Karmaṇy-evādhikāraste, mā phaleṣhu kadāchana.)
('You have the right to work, but not
to the fruits of your work.')

"When you hold ambition with love," he said, "you stop viewing others as competitors and start viewing them as collaborators. Love makes your work a contribution, not simply the sunk cost of acquiring rewards."

How Do We Bring Love Into Family Life?

Elina's expression softened and she asked, "How do we bring this back to our family? To Ishlin, to our parents, and the things we love?"

Advait's smile widened. "Family is the testing ground of love, but it's also where love is nurtured. Conscious love is born in the small, everyday interactions."

He outlined a few principles:

Presence: "When you are with your family, be completely there. Put down your phone. Look into their eyes. Listen."

Patience: "Remember that love isn't always easy. It takes patience, especially with those who test you the most."

Playfulness: "Don't take everything so seriously. Laugh, make things and bring joy together."

"In family life, love is often expressed as service: preparing tea for a parent, reading a bedtime story, or just asking, 'How are you?'" These little acts have a lot of power."

A Personal Love Ritual

Advait got up and lit an additional lamp next to the first. "A ritual is something that can ground love into your every day." It provides a moment of reflection, an omen of what matters most. Allow me to show you how to make your own."

1. Gratitude:

Purpose: Start your morning with love and intention.

Practice: (a) Every morning, find a quite space and spend five minutes sitting, (b) Think of three things you're grateful for, whether that's your partner, your family or just the breath in your lungs, and (c) Finish with the mantra: "***Today, I choose love.***"

2. Midday Connection:

Purpose: To slow down and check in with yourself when the workday is busy.

Practice: (a) Make a midday check-in alarm or reminder with your phone, (b) Take one deep self-compassionate breath and ask yourself, "***Am I currently acting from love?"***, (c)Otherwise, change your approach or your thinking.

3. Evening Reflection:

Purpose: End of Day Reflection with Mindfulness and Gratitude.

Practice: (a) Practice before bed with your partner or write alone in your journal, (b) Think about one loving thing you did or saw that day, (c) In case there were moments of conflict, quietly forgive yourself and each other.

The Heart Mandala (Private Practice)

That evening, Advait asked Ishaan and Elina to perform

a private ritual, call ***the Heart (or Love) Mandala***.

Preparation: (a) Find sand, petals, or pebbles in different colors., (b) Draw a small circle on the ground, wholeness of love.

Step 1: Setting Intentions: Everyone introduces an object they placed in the circle and shares one of their red lines, how they will let love in—work, family, or personal growth.

Step 2: Sharing Gratitude: Switch off expressing gratitude given what the other has brought into your life.

Step 3: Closing: Hold hands and say together: ***"May this mandala remind us that love is the center of all we do."***

Elina was calmed as they finished the ritual. "It's so simple, yet it feels ... sacred," she said.

Ishaan nodded. "It's a way to take this place, this feeling, with us."

Advait's Closing Wisdom

Near the end of the session, Advait spoke for the last time.

"Love is not a thing you find; it's a thing you make, moment to moment. When you infuse love into your work, your family, your community, you change not just your life but the lives of hundreds and thousands around you."

He quoted a verse from the *Vigyan Bhairav Tantra*:

"अन्तः प्रेमं भजतः शिवः।"
(Antaḥ premaṁ bhajataḥ śivaḥ.)
('When one embraces love within, they find divinity everywhere.')

But he said as they left, remember:

"The world will challenge you, distract you, even exhaust you. But love, it's always inside you, waiting to be chosen."

The words stayed suspended between Ishaan and Elina as they made their way back to their room.

"It's not just about us anymore," said Ishaan. "It's about how we perform for the world."

"And how we choose to love," Elina added. "Every day."

Overhead, the lamps at *Antara* glowed steadily in the approaching darkness—a reminder that love, once ignited, is a light capable of lighting up the world.

∞∞∞

Love as Liberation

The Final Frontier

Soft light fell upon *Antara* on the last day of December. The retreat was soaked in the stillness of the Western Ghats and seemed to suspend time itself as Elina and Ishaan readied themselves for a final session with Advait. It was a bittersweet morning — their hearts heavy at leaving, but lightened at the transformation they had made.

I still have to learn how to be a better person. He wore the same calm wisdom that had directed them through the days before, but his eyes had changed, and with them his sense of what they were — something more than the young couple in front of him, a life he could not comprehend.

"Today," Advait was starting, his voice filled with reverentis, "is the end of your time here, but not the end of your journey. You have come to understand love isn't just a feeling, a relationship, even an energy. It is liberation itself — the final frontier."

The Seeker Who Found Freedom

Advait put his feet on the floor, getting ready to tell the last story of their retreat. Once upon a time, there was a seeker named Arjun who roamed through forests and mountains in search of enlightenment for many years. He learned scriptures, meditated for hours and practiced austerities, yet his heart was still restless.

One day, Arjun met a wise sage sitting under a banyan tree. The sage emitted a sense of calmness that Arjun had not experienced before. Fall at his feet, Arjun pleaded, 'Master, what do I need to do to find liberation?

"The sage said to him, 'Who do you love?'

'What? Love?' Arjun asked, confused. 'E Enterer of the Essence, the one who seeks liberation, not of the worldly attachments.'

"The wise man smiled, 'One with liberation without love is like a bird without wings. The way of love; that's the end of the road. 'Go, love — not to have it, but to be it.'

"Arjun listened to the sage's advice with care. He went back to his village and then changed the way he lived. He took up afforestation, helped the sick and mended broken relations. Gradually, each act of love stripped away the walls he had built around himself. One day, when he was sitting under the same banyan tree, he felt that restlessness had left him. Love hadn't merely healed him — it had liberated him."

Advait paused, his eyes sparkling as he turned to Elina and Ishaan. "The sage's instruction to Arjun is the same I give you: Love is not the destination. It is the path itself. When you walk this path, release becomes a given"

Love As A Form Of Liberation

"As per the teachings of OSHO, love and freedom co-exist. He taught:

'*Love is true only when it gives you freedom.* Love is false when it binds you. The more love frees you, the closer you come to your true self.'

"This is how true love doesn't bind you to beliefs, roles, or attachments. It melts the ego, the sense of separation, and connects you with the infinite."

He quoted the *Bhagavad Gita*:

"यो मां पश्यति सर्वत्र, सर्वं च मयि पश्यति।"
(Yo māṁ paśyati sarvatra, sarvaṁ ca mayi paśyati.)
('He who sees me in all things, and all things in me, is never separated from me.')

"This verse speaks of the oneness that love exposes, a oneness that is the whole point of liberation," Advait explained.

The Resolve

Elina, her voice breaking despite the emotions in her eyes, said, "We came here broken. Not just as a couple, but as an individual. I don't think we knew what love could be."

Ishaan said, "But now we do. It's no longer merely about us. It's about how we live, how we love our son and our families and even the world around us. We want to take this knowledge and prove all the naysayers wrong — not out of defiance, but because we believe in what we've discovered here."

Advait smiled. "You don't have to prove anything to anyone. *Live in love, and the truth of your transformation will shine brighter than any words.*"

Ritual For The Year Of Love

And Advait gave a simple yet profound ritual that they could go forth with as they started their new lives.

Preparation: (a) At the stroke of midnight, light a candle together., and (b) Put a blank journal between you.

Step 1: Intentions: Each of you writes an intention for how you will embody love in the coming year — toward yourself, each other and the world.

Step 2: Affirmation: Read your intentions aloud, then together say: "This year, we choose love as our path and our purpose."

Step 3: Sealing the Ritual: Extinguish the candle together, marking closure to old habits, and set the journal somewhere it is visible so that you remember what you set out to do.

"This ritual," Advait said, "is not only for New Year's Eve. It is something you can do time and again if you ever want to reorient yourself to love."

The Final Moments At *Antara*

As the sun began to set Elina and Ishaan finally packed to leave from *Antara*. They followed Advait to the entrance of the retreat, bags in hand and hearts wide open.

Ishaan said, looking at Advait with gratitude. "You've given us more than we can ever repay."

Advait laid one hand on Ishaan's shoulder. "You owe me nothing. The highest gift you can offer is to live this knowledge — to *allow your love to transform not just your lives, but those whose lives you touch.*"

Tears welling up in her eyes, Elina hugged Advait. "Thank you. For everything."

Advait smiled gently. "Thank yourselves. You dared to seek,

to know, to change."

As they drove away, the retreat grew smaller in the rearview mirror, but its lessons loomed large in their minds. *Antara* was no longer just a place; it was a state of being—a reminder of what it meant to live in love.

Love As The Path

The final rays of sunlight bathed the retreat in gold as Advait returned to the pavilion. He lit the brass lamp once more, its flame steady against the encroaching darkness. His thoughts turned to Elina and Ishaan, now embarking on their own journey.

He whispered softly, as though to the universe itself:

"Love is not something you reach; it is something you become. When you choose love, you choose freedom. And in freedom, you find the infinite."

As the lamp's flame danced, it seemed to echo the truth of his words: Love, when fully embraced, is not an end but the ultimate beginning.

∞∞∞

From Retreat to Reality

Where Love Meets Life

Antara, the retreat was now behind them, but its lessons were reverberating deeply in Ishaan and Elina. The car purred gently as they drifted down the peaceful Western Ghats into the thrumming excitement of once-again meeting Ishlin, their son and Ishaan's parents, Madhav and Mohini.

Elina, next to Ishaan, nodded, gazing at the landscape rolling past, from becoming-hills to becoming-people. It was the first time she hadn't felt heavy-hearted in years. Ishaan's steady driving matched the silence, yet profound connection they had rediscovered in the days leading to this one. The space between them wasn't thick with words anymore; it was comfortably, longingly reflective.

At last, she spoke up. "Ishaan, what do you think we will say when your parents ask us how it went?"

Ishaan smiled and stared straight at the road. "I guess I'll say it wasn't what I expected; it was a whole lot more. "Advait didn't only make us talk about the idea of love, but also made us live and question it, see love for what it really is."

"Yes," Elina smiled. "It's as if we've lived a lifetime over these past ten days. Do you believe we need to put down in writing what we have learned? To remind ourselves in case life gets... chaotic again?"

"That's the right thing to do," Ishaan said. He looked at her with warmth. "Why don't we start now?"

Love Begins Within

"The first thing that hit me was Advait's perspective on self-love," Elina began. He helped me see that I was so obsessed with what we'd lost between us that I neglected myself."

"And he was right — if we can't love and accept ourselves, we'll always look to the other person to fill that void." Remember to honor myself as much as I honor you."

They recalled Advait's words:

"True love begins within. You have unlimited love to offer when you are overflowing with love for yourself."

Vulnerability Is A Strength

Ishaan chuckled softly. "Do you all remember the eye-gazing exercise? I figured I would suck at it."

"You probably weren't," Elina said, smiling. "It was tough at first, though. Just looking into your eyes, seeing all of the things that we had not yet told each other ... it broke me, but in the best way."

Advait had talked about *vulnerability being the basis of intimacy.*

"Fortified walls protect, but walls also isolate. True connection only happens when you let yourself be seen, flaws and all.'

"We just have to keep doing that," Ishaan said. "Inviting each other in when it's uncomfortable."

Boundaries Are Acts Of Love

Elina reclined her voice thoughtful. "The lesson about boundaries shocked me. I used to think that saying no was selfish. But Advait helped me understand it differently: It's not about pushing people away; it's about carving out space for respect and understanding."

Ishaan nodded. "And they go both ways. I realized that I've been crossing your boundaries without even noticing. "I'll do better to honor them."

The words of Advait echoed in their mind:

"Boundaries are not barriers; they are bridges. They reveal where love can take root."

Love Is A Practice

"Love is not only what we feel in the good times," Ishaan said. "It's a thing we intentionally practice every day, in all moments, even in hard times."

At *Antara*, Elina thought about their time together. "They reminded me that love is built in the small, consistent acts — the rituals, the breathing exercises, even just holding hands and sharing a moment of gratitude... these are the things that bring you closer together throughout your life."

Advait had always stressed that,

"Love is not an emotion to fall into; it is a practice to rise into. It is cultivated through presence, intention, and action."

The Balance Of Masculine And Feminine

Elina laughed softly. "I didn't think that I would like the sun and moon exercises as much as I do. They were so easy, but they made me feel ... balanced."

"Me too," Ishaan agreed. "I was always in my 'doer' mode, chasing goals, but Advait showed me the power in slowing down, being receptive, and just... simply being."

They recalled the ritual of revering each other's energies, a marriage of the Taoist idea of yin and yang and the Tantric balance of Shiva and Shakti.

"When both masculine and feminine energies are balancing each other within you and in between you, love comes about naturally."

Communication Is Sacred

Elina sighed. "I think that listening bowl exercise was a pivotal moment for me. "For the first time in a long time, I felt like you actually listened to me, like not just the words coming out my mouth, but what was behind them."

"And I recognized how many times I'd been listening to respond, not to understand," Ishaan said. "That has to change."

Advait's instructions had been explicit:

"The words are powerful, but the magic of communication is in the spaces between the words. Listen not just with your ears, you know, listen with your heart."

Love Transcends The Personal

As they neared the outskirts of Pune, Ishaan spoke softly. "The cosmic unity meditation ... it's hard to put into words, but it made me feel so small and so infinite at the same time."

Elina nodded. "It's humbling, isn't it? To understand that our love is not solely between you and I — it is part of something larger."

Advait's last words echoing in their minds:

"When the love goes beyond the personal that love heals not just two hearts but the world."

Looking Ahead

With the approach of Kalyani Nagar, the streets surrounding Madhav and Mohini's bungalow were now familiar. Ishaan reduced the speed of the car & Elina gave him some looks of quiet determination.

"We have come a long way, Ishaan," she said. "But now the real journey begins."

He smiled, extended his hand toward her. "And we'll walk it together."

The bungalow appeared, its warm lights glowing in the dusk. Their son Ishlin would be waiting inside, along with Madhav and Mohini, to greet them home. But now it would not simply be a return to their physical home — it would signify a new chapter, one that would build on the lessons learned at *Antara*.

When Ishaan parked the car and turned the engine off, he looked over to Elina and said, "Let's make Advait proud. Let's make us proud."

Elina smiled, her eyes shining with hope. “Let’s.”

They got out of the car, prepared to embrace not only their family, but a future of love, presence, and purpose.

∞∞∞

Epilogue

Love is a Living Practice!

As the final pages of this journey come to a close, I invite you to pause for a moment—not to end, but to reflect. Stories, like love, never truly end. They evolve, grow, and continue with every choice we make.

The story of Ishaan, Elina, and Advait may have reached its conclusion, but their journey is far from over. Like all of us, they will face new challenges, navigate new uncertainties, and encounter moments of doubt. But there is a difference now—they have the tools, the awareness, and most importantly, the courage to face it together.

I didn't write their story just for them. It was written for you.
Whether you see a reflection of yourself in Ishaan, in Elina, or even in Advait, the heart of this story belongs to you. Their doubts, fears, moments of surrender, and breakthroughs mirror the experiences that countless couples, partners, and seekers face every day. Their story is a reminder that no relationship is perfect, but every relationship is perfect for growth.

For the benefit of my readers who have skipped some of the pages and paratrooped on this section, I summarize the seven key takeaways from ***Love Transcended: Where Love Evolves into Consciousness.***

1. Love Is Not a Destination:

It's a Path We Walk Every Day. Love is not something we "achieve" or "acquire." It is not a prize, a status, or a guarantee. It is a daily practice, a choice we make again and again. Just as Ishaan and Elina learned to nurture love through vulnerability, presence, and patience, so too can we. Love does not happen to us; it happens through us.

"Love is not something you find. It is something you become."

2. Self-love is the foundation of every other love :

Through her own journey, Elina learned that self-love is not selfish—it is essential. We cannot give love from an empty heart. When we neglect our self-worth, we become desperate for validation from others, turning love into a transaction. But when we cultivate compassion for ourselves, we become whole. With this wholeness, love flows freely.
If you take away just one message from this story, let it be this:

"You are worthy of love, not because of what you do, but because of who you are."

3. Boundaries Are Not Barriers—They Are Bridges:

For years, Ishaan and Elina struggled with boundaries —not because they didn't care, but because they didn't know how to articulate them. Setting boundaries can feel uncomfortable, but it is a profound act of love. Boundaries are not walls to keep people out; they are bridges to deeper understanding.

A simple "no" spoken with love and clarity can save relationships, just as a clear "yes" can foster trust.

"Boundaries honor each partner's individuality while nurturing the shared space of togetherness. Remember, you can say "no" and still be kind."

4. Intimacy is built in vulnerability:

Many of us hide parts of ourselves, fearing that our flaws will drive others away. But true intimacy is not born from perfection—it is born from vulnerability. When Ishaan and Elina engaged in eye-gazing, they were not merely looking into each other's eyes; they were gazing into each other's unspoken fears, dreams, and humanity.

When you strip away the armor and let your partner see you fully, you are saying, "Here I am. All of me." And in that rawness, love deepens.

"To be vulnerable is to be brave. To be brave is to be free."

5. Masculine and feminine energies exist in all of us:

The balance of Shiva (masculine) and Shakti (feminine) is not just a poetic ideal; it is a reflection of the forces within us. We each hold both energies within ourselves. Ishaan discovered that embracing the calm, receptive nature of his feminine energy did not make him weaker —it made him whole.

Whether you identify as a man, woman, or beyond, remember that you are not one or the other. You are both. The world has conditioned us to favor logic, reason, and action (masculine), but love also requires intuition, surrender, and stillness (feminine).

"Harmony is not about balance. It is about flow."

6. Healing Begins With Forgiveness:

If there is one thing that binds us to the past, it is unforgiveness. Advait taught Ishaan and Elina that forgiveness is not about pardoning the one who hurt us—it is about setting ourselves free. Whether you are holding on to the mistakes of your partner, your parents, or yourself, forgiveness is a radical act of love.

Ask yourself:

> Who am I still blaming?
> What would happen if I let go of the blame today?

"The moment you forgive, you no longer live in the past. You return to the present, which is where love resides."

7. Love transcends the personal:

Perhaps the most profound message of this book is that love is not just about "you and me."

"Love extends beyond the realm of romance. It transcends relationships, flowing into every part of life. "

Ishaan and Elina experienced this shift during the cosmic unity meditation, where they realized that love is a universal force that moves through everything and everyone.

This book is not just about romantic love. It is about universal love. It is about the love we cultivate for our children, our friends, our communities, and even strangers. As we see love as universal rather than "personal," we awaken to a higher state.

"When love transcends the personal, it becomes a force that heals the world."

This Is Not the End—This Is the Beginning.

This story is not a magic pill. It is not a quick-fix solution.It is an invitation.

It is an invitation for you to take the first step. To look within yourself and ask:

Where am I withholding love?
Where am I afraid of love?
Where can I bring more love into my daily life?

The narrative of Ishaan, Elina, and Advait mirrors your personal journey. Their struggles are your struggles. Their questions are your questions. If you're willing to act, their growth can become your own.

If this book stirred something within you—a realization, a question, or even a quiet sense of possibility—I invite you to continue the dialogue.

I do not claim to have all the answers. No one does. But I do believe that answers emerge when we ask the right questions.
If you wish to go deeper, to discuss your own unique journey of love and self-discovery, I welcome you to reach out. I believe in the power of dialogue, and I believe in the power of personal transformation through connection.

You are not alone. You are never alone.

Reach out if you need guidance, reflection, or love—not just their love, but yours. Let us walk this path together.

As you close this book, I leave you with one final thought.

Love is not something you chase. Love is not something you wait for. Love is something you awaken within.

You have the opportunity to live with love every day, with every breath. Love is present not only in your romantic relationships but also in every moment, every word, and every decision you make.

This is not the end of a story. This is the beginning of a love that transcends all boundaries.

With love and infinite gratitude,

Vishwas

∞∞∞

LOVE TRANSCENCED
Where Love Evolves into Consciousness.

What if love could heal, transform, and transcend?

Ishaan and Elina, a modern couple on the verge of losing their connection, embark on a transformative journey to Antara, a secluded retreat in the Western Ghats of India. Guided by Advait, a former scientist turned sage, they confront their fears, rediscover intimacy, and awaken to the boundless potential of love.

Blending timeless teachings from Vedic, Buddhist, Taoist, and Tantric traditions with practical tools for personal growth, "Love Transcended" is a story of redemption and self-discovery that resonates across cultures and walks of life.

Through engaging storytelling, profound insights, and actionable exercises, this book offers readers a roadmap to cultivate love—not just as a feeling, but as a transformative force that connects us to ourselves, each other, and the universe.

Perfect for readers seeking deeper relationships, personal healing, and spiritual growth.

The Author:

Vishwas Chavan is a visionary author, spiritual mentor, and speaker, known for blending ancient wisdom with modern insights to inspire love, consciousness, and growth. A scientist, academician, and futurist, he bridges science and spirituality offering transformative perspectives on human potential.

∞∞∞

www.ingramcontent.com/pod-product-compliance
Lightning Source LLC
Chambersburg PA
CBHW062141160726
48282CB00027B/896
* 9 7 8 9 3 3 4 1 8 1 9 5 1 *